JIMI HENDRIX STYLE

Guitar Book with Online Video & Audio Access

Taught By
Jody Worrell

To access Online Audio & Video for this course, go to the following web address:

http://cvls.com/extras/jhs/

Watch & Learn

Copyright 2018 by Watch & Learn, Inc., First Edition
ALL RIGHTS RESERVED. Any copying, arranging, or adapting of this work without the consent of the owner is an infringement of copyright.

Lick 4

Lick 4 uses lots of hammer-ons and double stops.

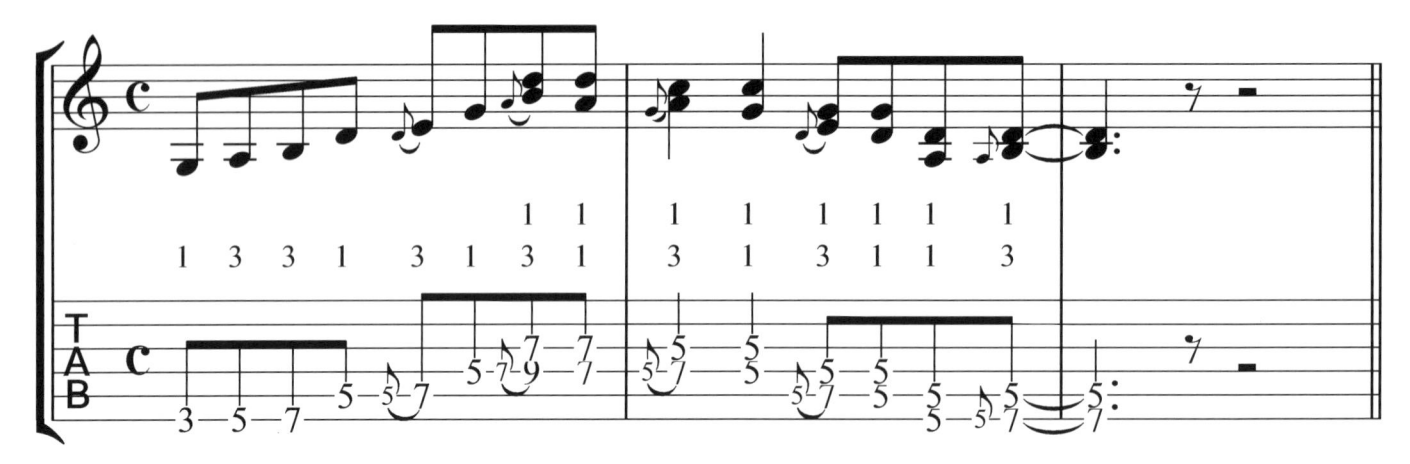

Lick 5

This lick is played on the 1st and 3rd strings with slides on the 3rd string.

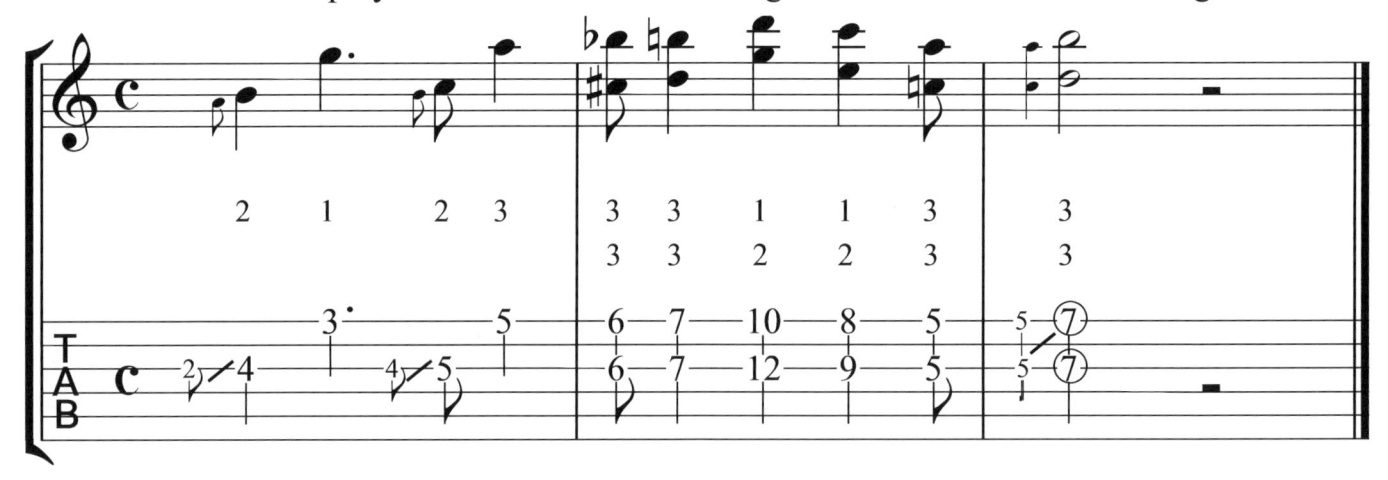

Playing With Jam Track

Now we'll play all five licks along with the audio track in a random order. When you get to the point where you can pick and choose them as you like, you're well on your way to owning the licks and you can use them in your day to day playing.

To access Audio & Video for this course, go to this web address:
http://cvls.com/extras/jhs/

The Author

Jody Worrell has been a professional performer and teacher in the Atlanta area for over 30 years. He has recorded and appeared on stage domestically and internationally with such artists as Lyle Lovett, Mitch Ryder and the Detroit Wheels, Badfinger, Delbert McClinton, Phil Collins, The Marvelettes, The Drifters, The Tokens, The Crystals, Derek Trucks, and many others. Jody plays all styles on demand, but always returns to the blues, taking an approach which is based in tradition, but always seeking to expand harmonic boundaries. He also has to his credit four of the many Watch & Learn products: *Let's Jam! CD Blues & Rock Vol. 3*, *Let's Jam! CD Country Vol. 2*, *Let's Jam! Blues Standards*, and *Blues Licks & Solos*.

Jody studied classical guitar briefly with the legendary John Sutherland, but attributes his playing mostly to hard work, open-mindedness to diverse types of music, and to the indelible mark left by long-time teacher, mentor and friend, Merrill Dilbeck.

Jody has produced almost three hundred video lessons on blues, rock, and country for GuitarCompass.com.

How To Use The Book & Video

Step 1 - Watch the Video while following along with the book. Play along with the Video on your guitar. Replay each chapter on the Video until you are comfortable playing along with it.

Step 2 - When you are comfortable with a lesson or piece of music, try playing along with the audio track for each lesson on the Video. You'll find these on the Chapter Menus. Try expanding your horizons a little and stretch out your technique. Don't be afraid to experiment.

Step 3 - Go back to the book & Video and play along to make sure you're on the right track.

TABLE OF CONTENTS

	Page
Tablature, & Techniques	1
Tablature	2
Hammer-ons & Pull-offs	3
Slides & Bends	4
Jimi Hendrix Style Major Licks	5
Lick 1	6
Licks 2 & 3	7
Licks 4 & 5	8
Playing With Jam Track	8
Jimi Hendrix Style Bends	9
Lick 1	9
Licks 2 & 3	10
Licks 4 & 5	11
Playing With Jam Track	11
Jimi Hendrix Style Ballad Solo 1	12
Phrase 1	12
Phrases 2 & 3	13
Phrase 4	14
Whole Solo	14-15
Jimi Hendrix Style Ballad Solo 2	16
Phrase 1	16
Phrases 2 & 3	17
Phrase 4	18
Whole Solo	18-19
Jimi Hendrix Style Ballad Solo 3	20
Phrase 1	20
Phrases 2 & 3	21
Phrase 4	22
Whole Solo	22-23
Jimi Hendrix Style Ballad Solo 4	24
Phrase 1	24
Phrases 2 & 3	25
Phrase 4	26
Whole Solo	26-27
Where To Go Next	28

About This Course

Jimi Hendrix Style is the third installment in the *In The Style Of The Legends Series*. All courses include two full length DVDs packed full of famous licks and solos as interpreted by Jody Worrell. The courses are in the style of legendary guitarists such as Stevie Ray Vaughan, Eric Clapton, Jimi Hendrix, B.B. King, David Gilmour, and more.

Each lick and solo is broken down and the techniques and timing of each phrase is totally explained and played several times. Close-ups and split screens are used to make learning even clearer. In addition to the video instruction, there are full band practice tracks allowing the students to practice with a professional band anytime they want to perfect their timing and technique.

A book is included with the two DVDs that has standard music notation and tablature for everything that is taught. The type face is large for ease of viewing.

The *In The Style Of The Legends Series* is based on content developed during 15 years of producing lessons for GuitarCompass.com which have been viewed by millions of guitarists. If you like these DVDs and want more high quality lessons, go to FreeGuitarVideos.com to see their Free Lessons and Premium Lessons.

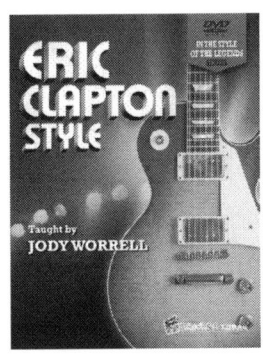

To access Online Audio & Video for this course, go to the following web address:
http://cvls.com/extras/jhs/

Fender®, and the distinctive headstock design commonly found on Fender® guitars, are registered trademarks of Fender Musical Instruments Corporation, and used herein with express written permission. All rights reserved.

TABLATURE & TECHNIQUES

Tablature

This book is written in both tablature and standard music notation. We will explain tablature because it is easy to learn if you are teaching yourself and because a lot of popular guitar music is available in tablature.

Tablature is a system for writing music that shows the proper string and fret to play. In guitar tablature, each line represents a string on the guitar. If the string is to be fretted, the fret number is written on the appropriate line. Otherwise a 0 is written. Study the examples below until you understand them thoroughly.

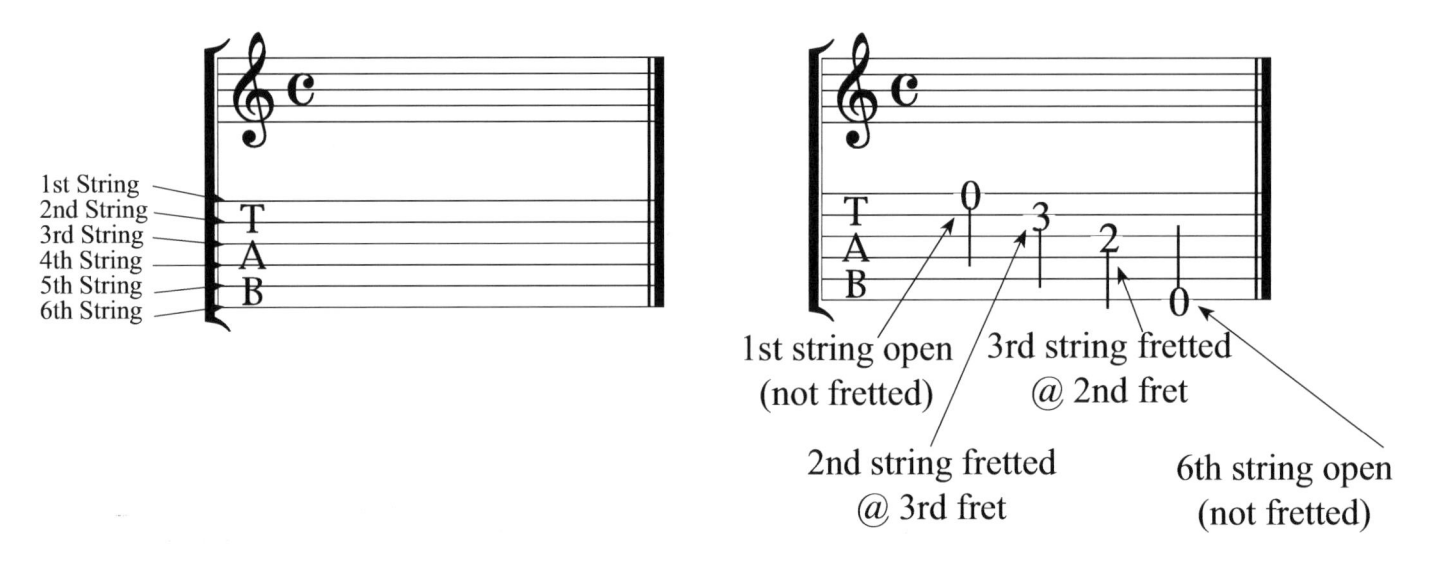

1st String
2nd String
3rd String
4th String
5th String
6th String

1st string open (not fretted)
2nd string fretted @ 3rd fret
3rd string fretted @ 2nd fret
6th string open (not fretted)

The music will be divided into two sets of lines (staffs).

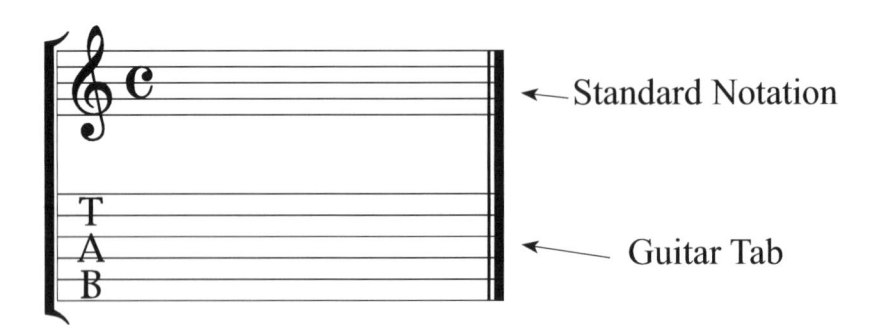

← Standard Notation

← Guitar Tab

Techniques

Here are some fundamental techniques that are used this course.

Hammer-ons & Pull-offs

When playing a hammer-on, pick the first note, then hammer-on with a finger on your left hand. You will need to be on the tip of the finger and strike the note with velocity and accuracy.

When playing a pull-off, again pick the first note, then pull-off with a finger on your left hand. Once again, use the tip of the finger. The finger you are pulling off to needs to hold the string stable during the pull off.

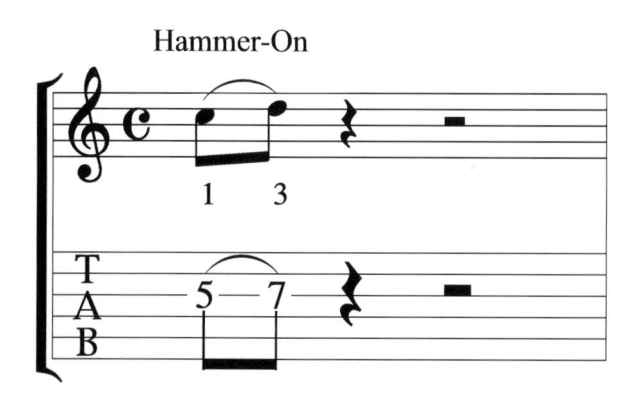

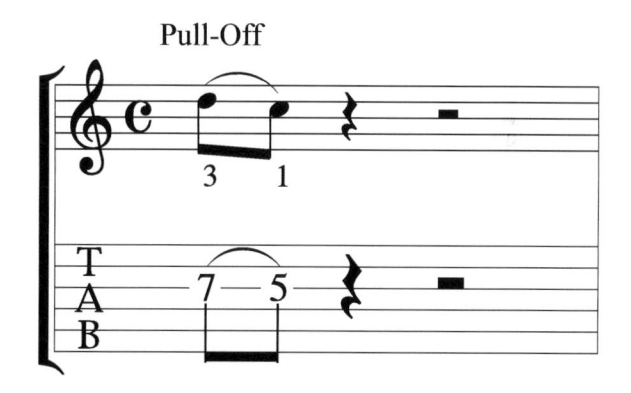

Hammer-on & Pull-off Combination

This technique starts by picking the first note, hammering on, and then pulling off back to the first note.

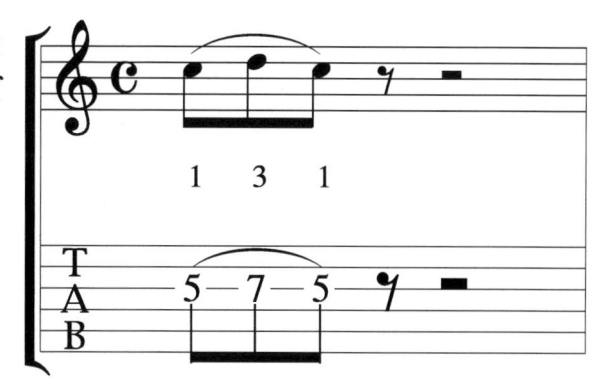

Slides

A slide means you pick a note and slide into another. Slides can move up or down and can be phrased many different ways.

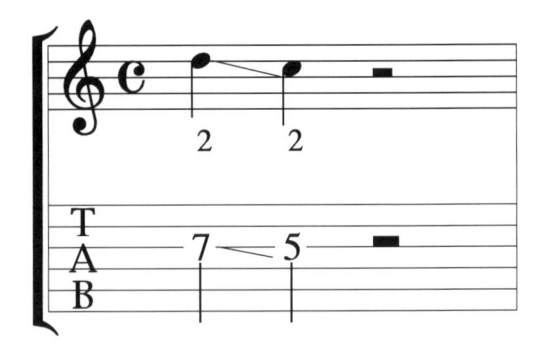

Slides From An Undetermined Note

This slide usually starts a fret or two away but sometimes further. It does not stay at the starting point long enough for the listener to really tell where it starts.

Double Stop Slides

This is a slide involving two notes. It is important that both fingers move evenly across the frets.

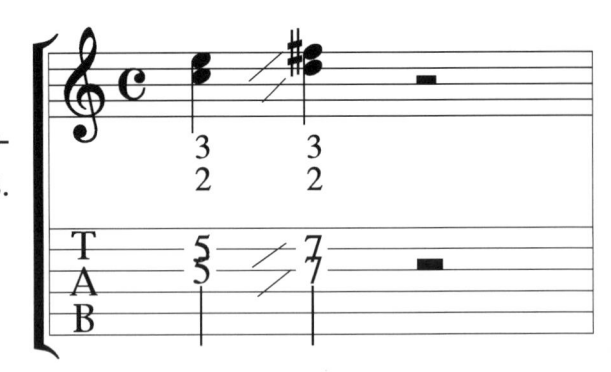

Bends

When playing a bend, use all the fingers that are available to help execute the bend. For example, use the third finger to bend the note, the second finger on the same string helping to bend the note, and the first finger to mute the string above it.

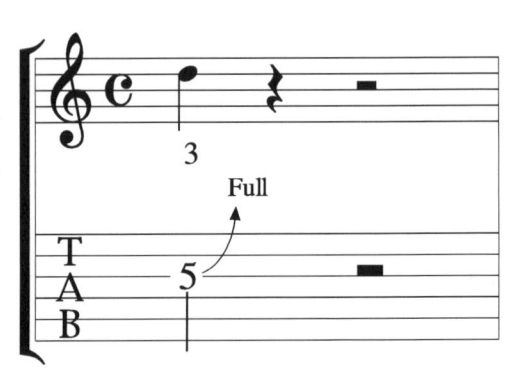

4

JIMI HENDRIX STYLE LICKS & SOLOS

Jimi Hendrix Style Major Licks

We'll learn five licks in the style of Jimi Hendrix capturing some of his trademark "clean tone" hammer-ons and slides using the double stop intervals he used throughout his work. The Video will cover some of the music theory behind each lick as well as give you an opportunity to trade the licks back and forth in a jam situation. All of these licks are in the key of G and we'll be playing a rocking G Chord groove from *Let's Jam! Blues & Rock Vol. 3*.

Lick 1

Start with a hammer-on on the 2nd string while holding down the 3rd fret on the 1st string.

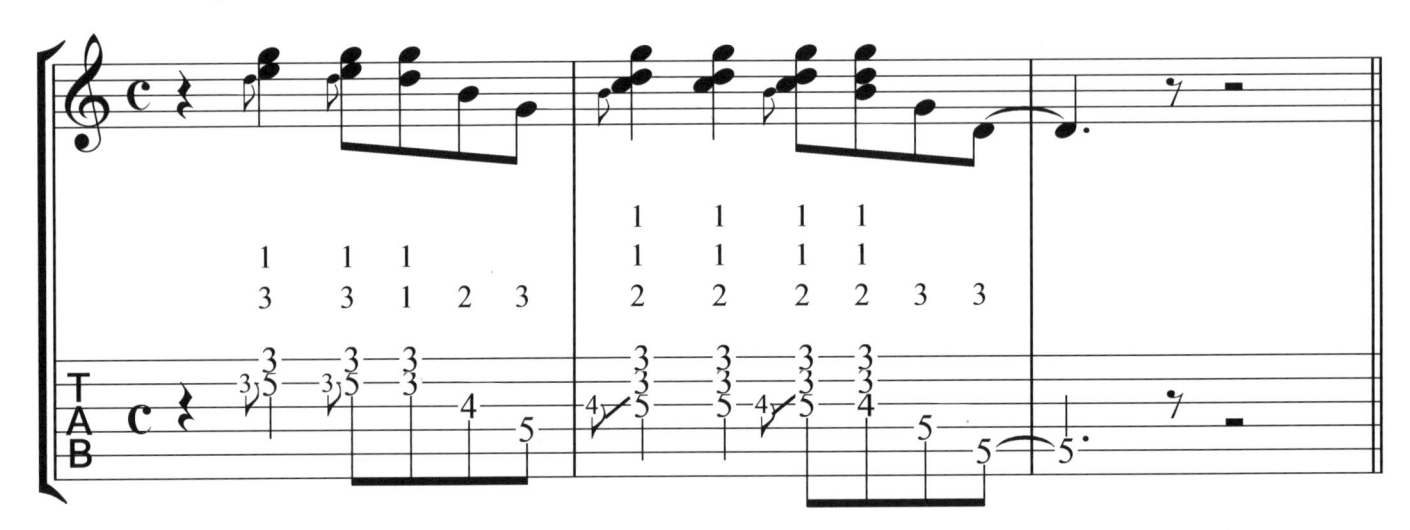

Demo

Each phrase will be played along with a backing track at the correct speed.

Trading Licks

Each lick will be traded back & forth. I'll play it first, then leave space for you to play it right after so you can compare your tone, timing, and articulation. Take your time and work on this section until you can play it perfectly all three times through.

Video & Audio Access

To access Audio & Video for this course, go to this web address:
http://cvls.com/extras/jhs/

Lick 2

We'll use the same format for each lick. First each lick will be taught in detail. Next it will be played at full speed along with a backing track. Then it will be traded back and forth, leaving space for you to play right after me. Note the three Video chapter markers so you can find the exact locations on the Video.

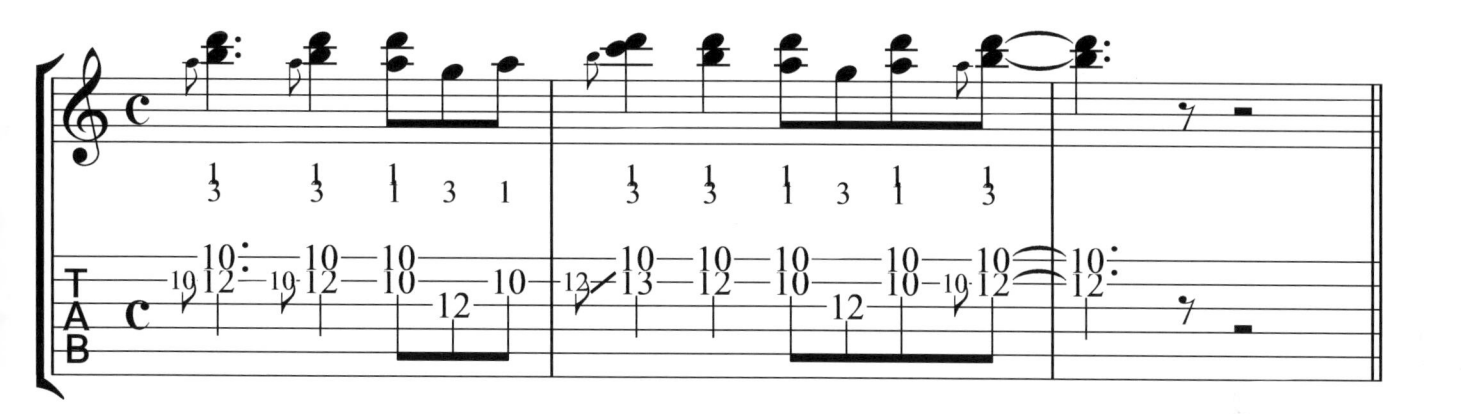

Lick 3

Lick 3 uses double stop slides that are a fourth apart. Listen to the Video for an explanation.

Note: You'll get the most from these lessons by taking your time and practicing each lick until you've mastered it. That's when you'll really be able to retain the licks and bring them into your day to day playing.

Jimi Hendrix Style Bends

We'll learn five more licks focusing on Jimi's trademark bending techniques. I'll teach you how to play each lick in detail making sure you understand how to properly play the bends. We'll play these licks over a track of E7 excepted from *Let's Jam! CD Blues & Rock Vol. 3*.

Lick 1

This lick uses the minor pentatonic with bends in the key of E.

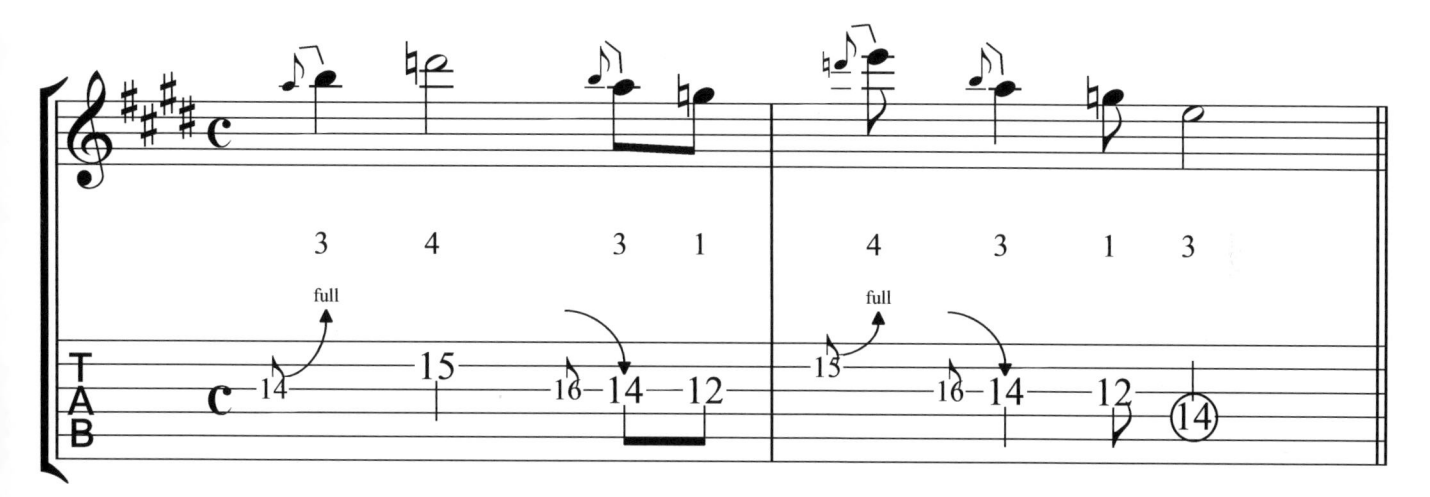

Demo

Each phrase will be played along with a backing track at the correct speed.

Trading Licks

Each lick will be traded back & forth. I'll play it first, then leave space for you to play it right after so you can compare your tone, timing, and articulation. Take your time and work on this section until you can play it perfectly all three times through.

Video & Audio Access

To access Audio & Video for this course, go to this web address:
http://cvls.com/extras/jhs/

Lick 2

This lick has lots of bending and sliding on one string.

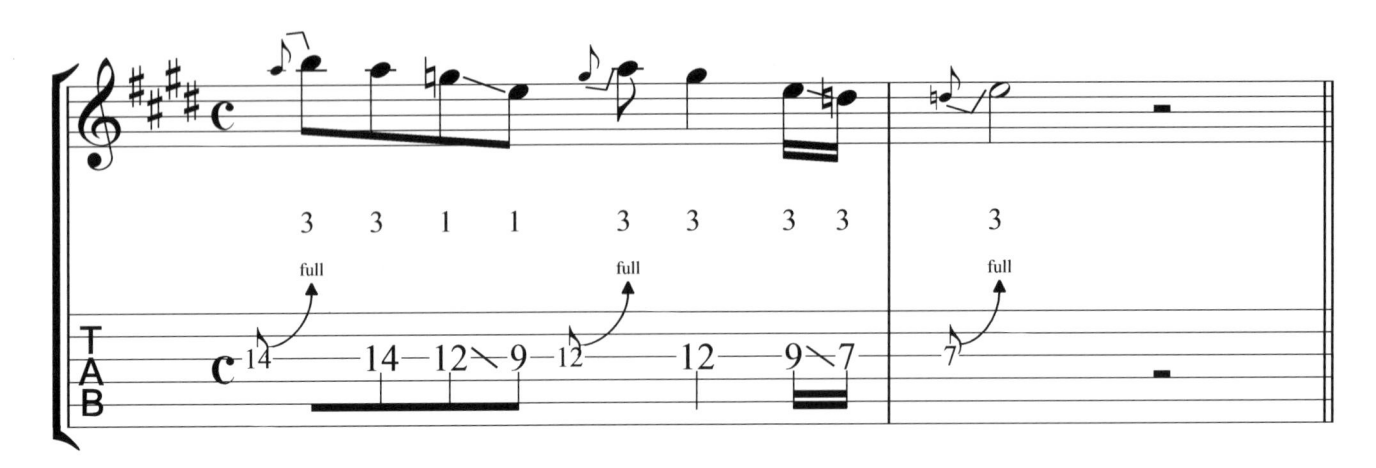

Lick 3

Lick 3 starts with a classic blues & rock lick.

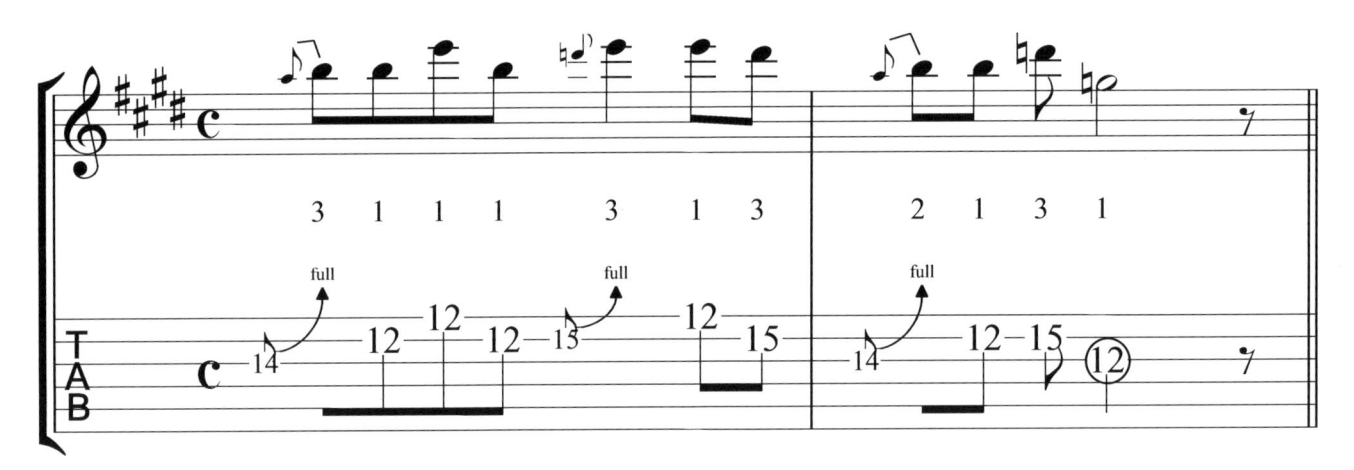

Note: Another great drill is to play the licks with me as well as in between in the trading section. Try this for all five licks in this section.

Lick 4

Watch the Video for an explanation of bending the 2nd and 3rd strings together.

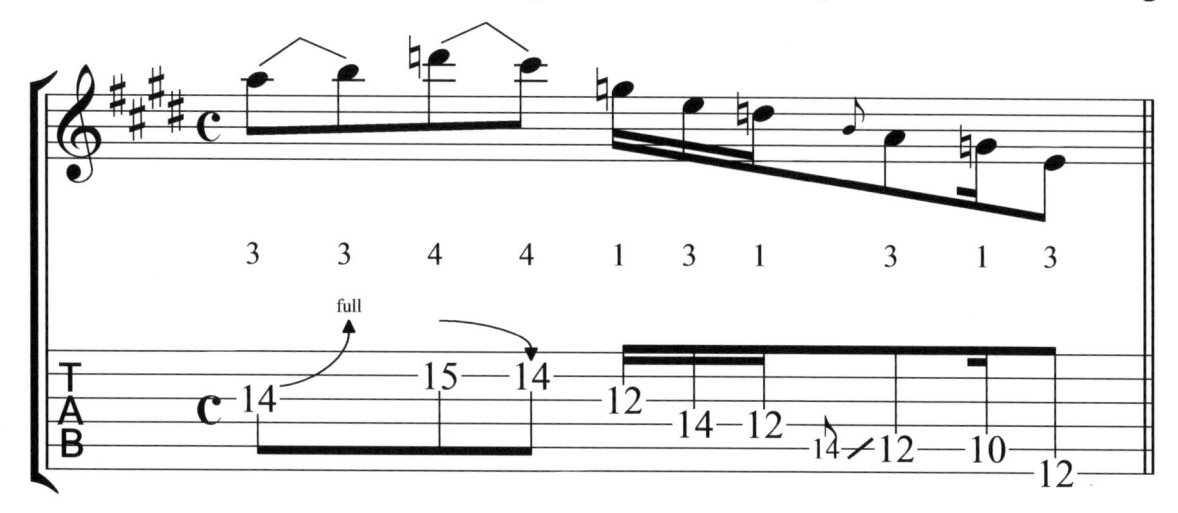

Lick 5

Similar to Lick 1, bend up on one string and bend down on another string.

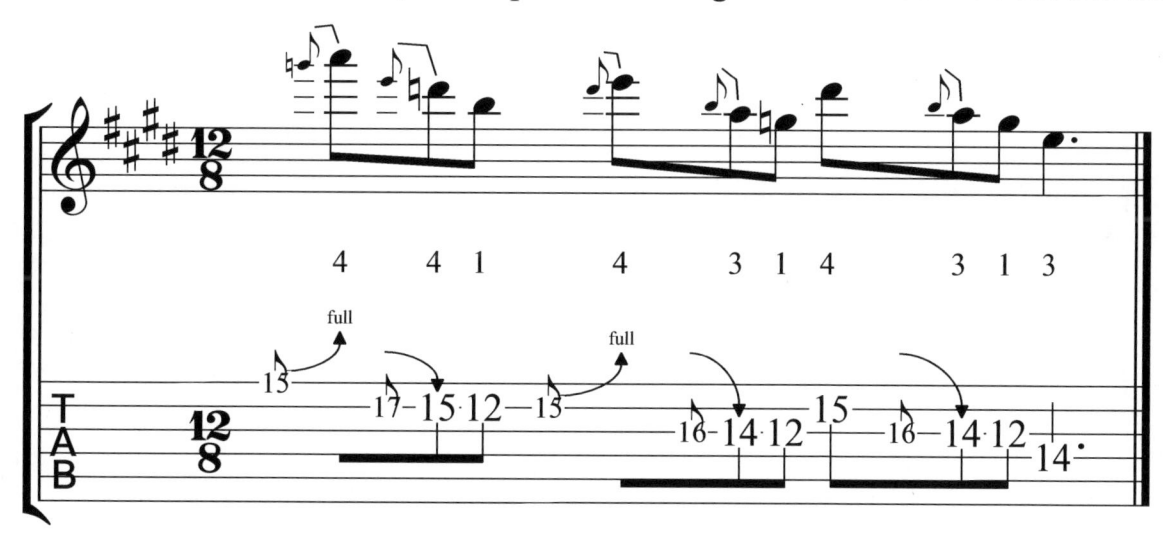

Playing With Jam Track

Now we'll play all five licks along with the audio track in a random order. When you get to the point where you can pick and choose them as you like, you're well on your way to owning the licks and you can use them in your day to day playing.

To access Audio & Video for this course, go to this web address:
http://cvls.com/extras/jhs/

Jimi Hendrix Style Ballad Solo 1

This is a 16 bar solo in the style of Jimi Hendrix. In songs like *Little Wing*, Jimi showed that he could create soaring and dramatic solos in a ballad setting. I'll walk you through playing the long sustained bent notes that Jimi used to help achieve this sound. After you've learned the guitar solo, you'll have the opportunity to practice along with a rhythm track. This solo is played over an Em groove audio track from *Let's Jam! CD Blues & Rock Volume 3*. We will start by playing the complete solo along with the jam track and then break the solo into four phrases.

Phrase 1

This starts with a whole step bend with vibrato. Watch the Video for details.

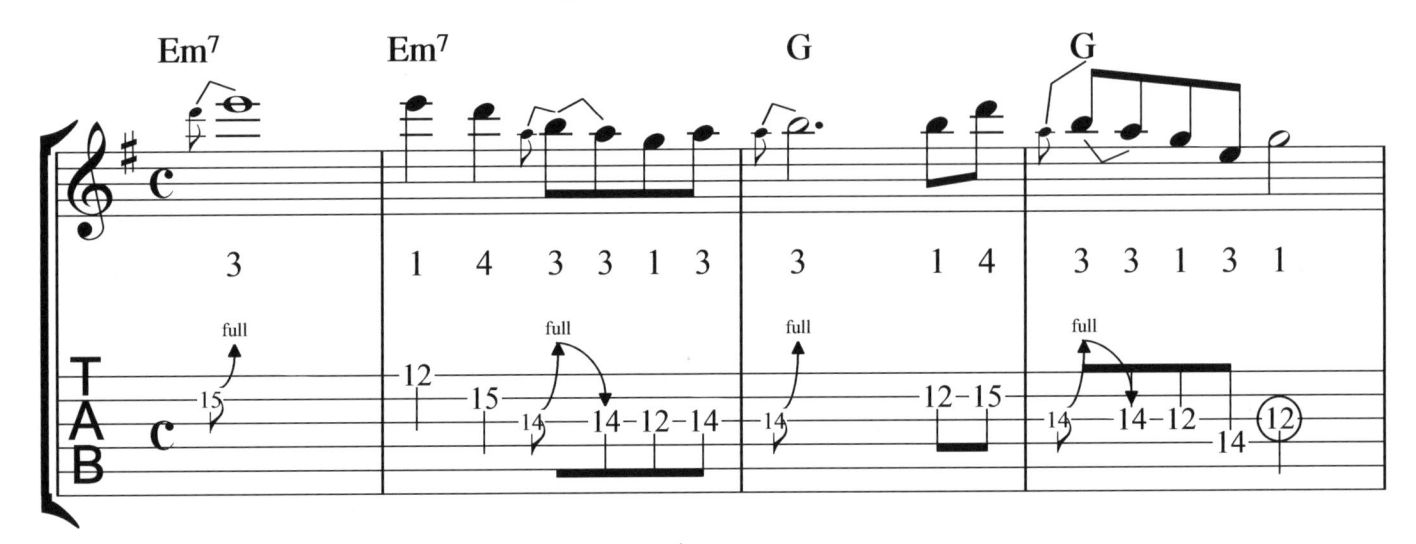

Demo

Each phrase will be played along with a backing track at the correct speed.

Trading Licks

Each lick will be traded back & forth. I'll play it first, then leave space for you to play it right after so you can compare your tone, timing, and articulation. Take your time and work on this section until you can play it perfectly all three times through.

Video & Audio Access

To Access Audio & Video for this course, go to this web address:
http://cvls.com/extras/jhs/

Phrase 2

Phrase 2 starts with a hammer-on from the 12th fret to the 14th fret on the 3rd string.

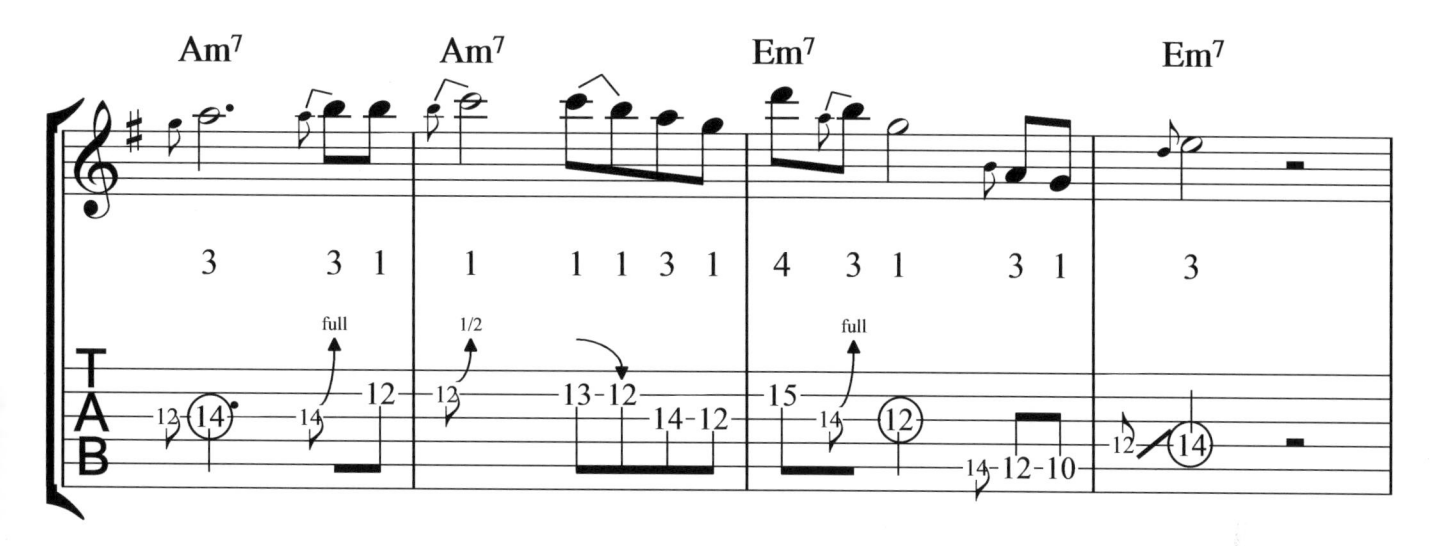

Phrase 3

Phrase 3 starts with a classic blues & rock lick.

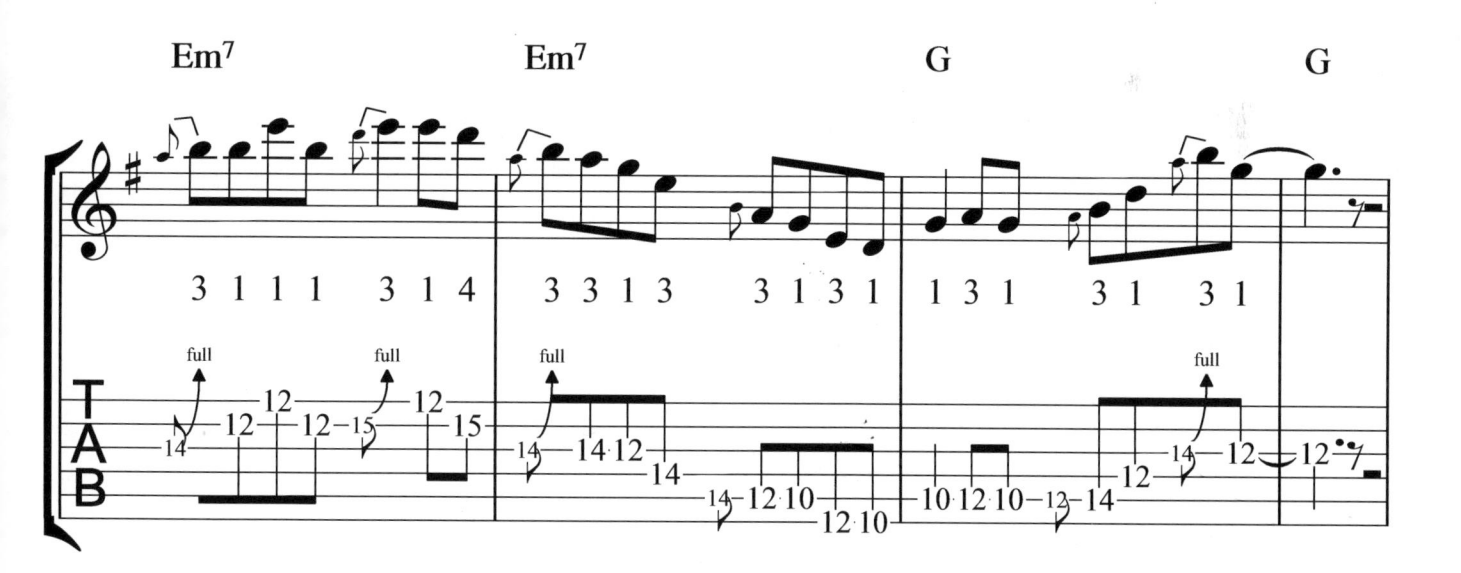

Phrase 4

Listen to the Video to understand how to separate the sound of the first two notes.

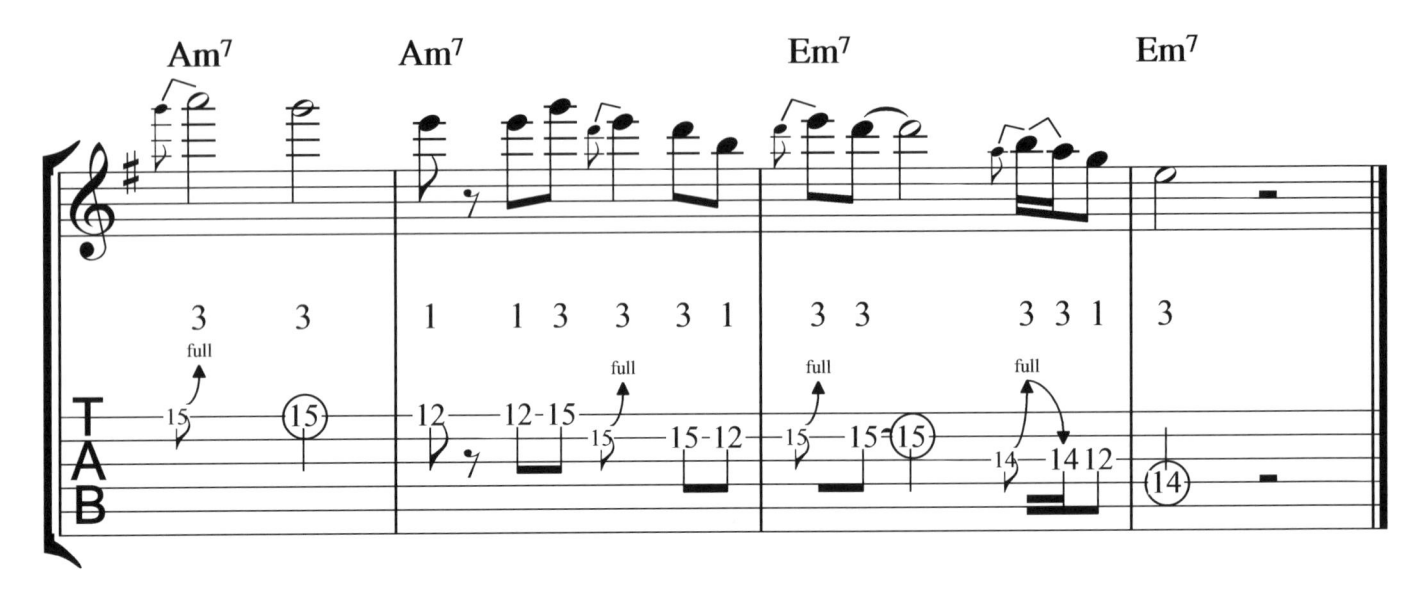

Playing With The Jam Track

Play the complete solo along with the jam track. You can access the file from the following web address:

http://cvls.com/extras/jhs/

Hendrix Style Ballad Solo 1

by Jody Worrell

Phrase 1

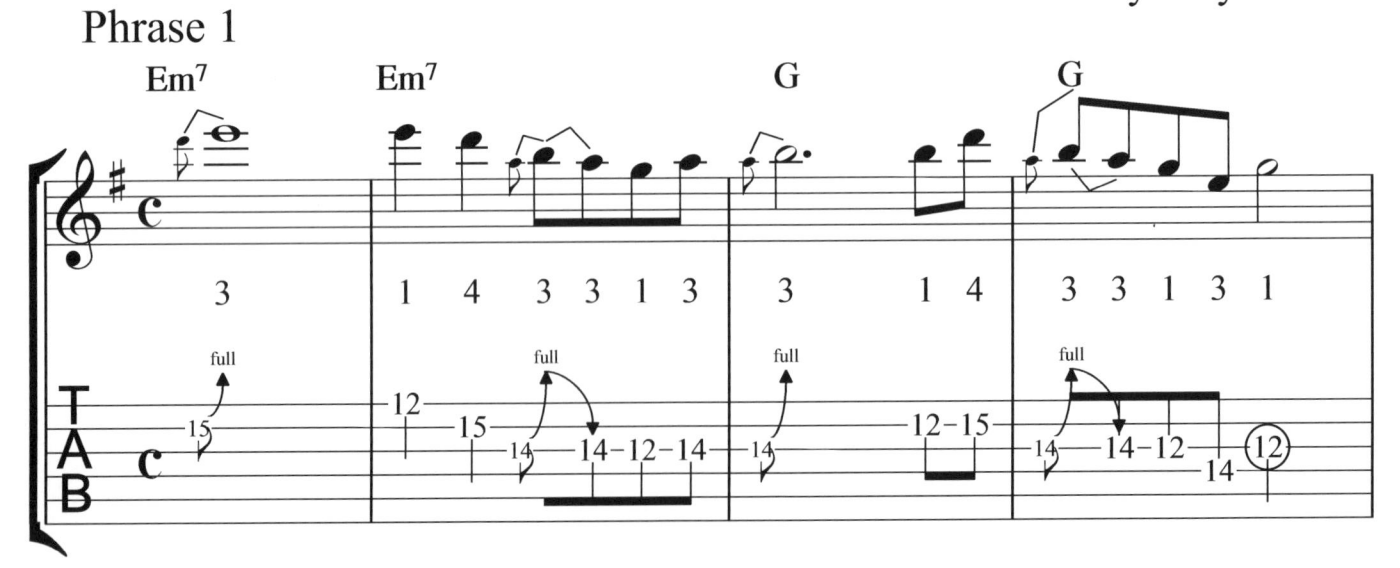

14

Phrase 2

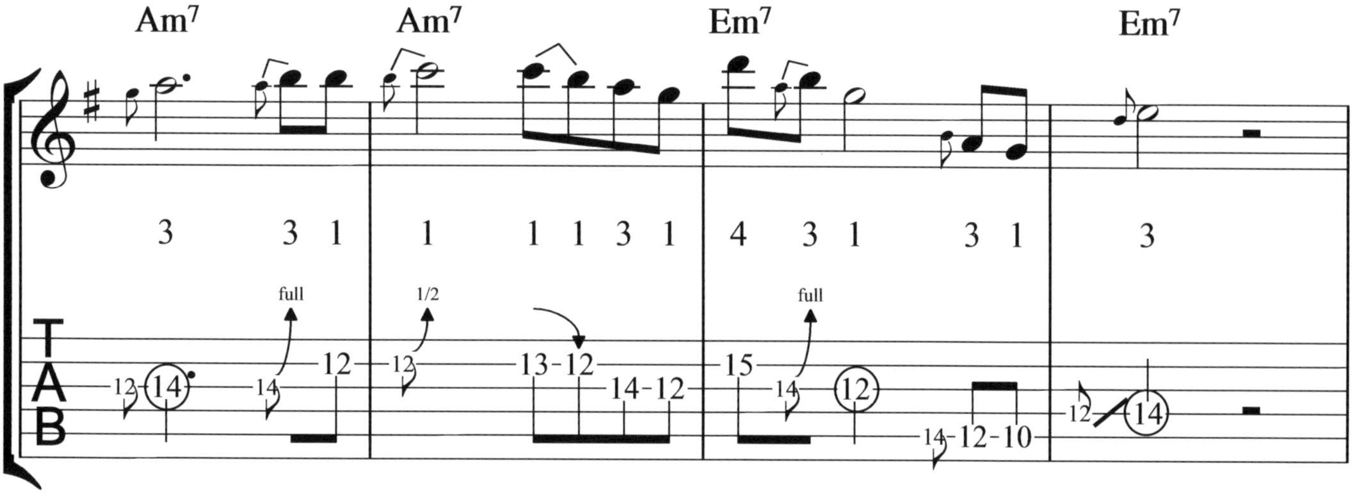

Phrase 3

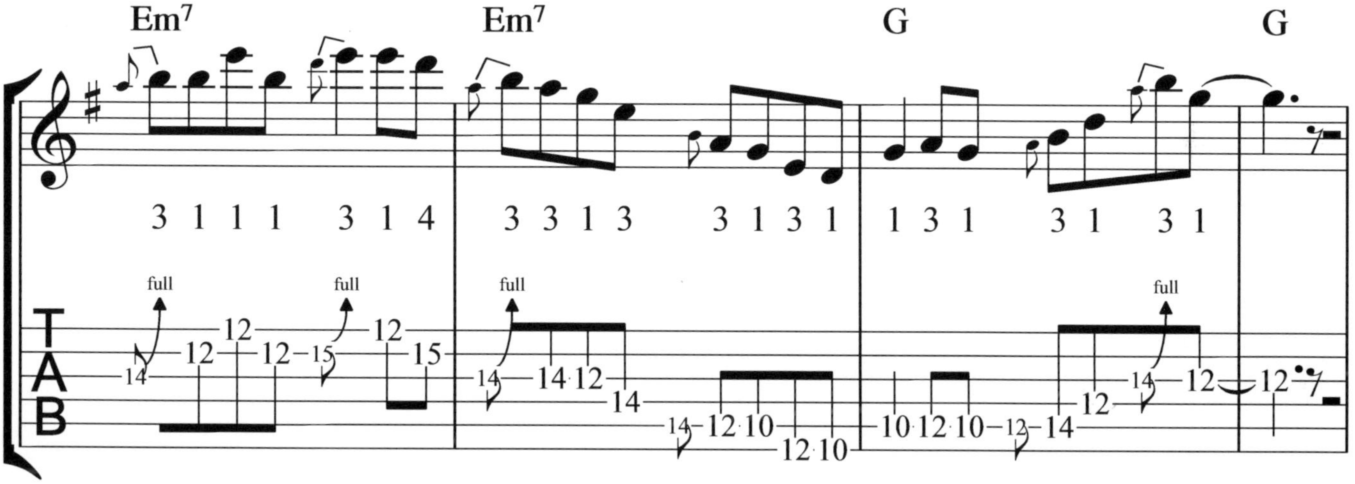

Phrase 4

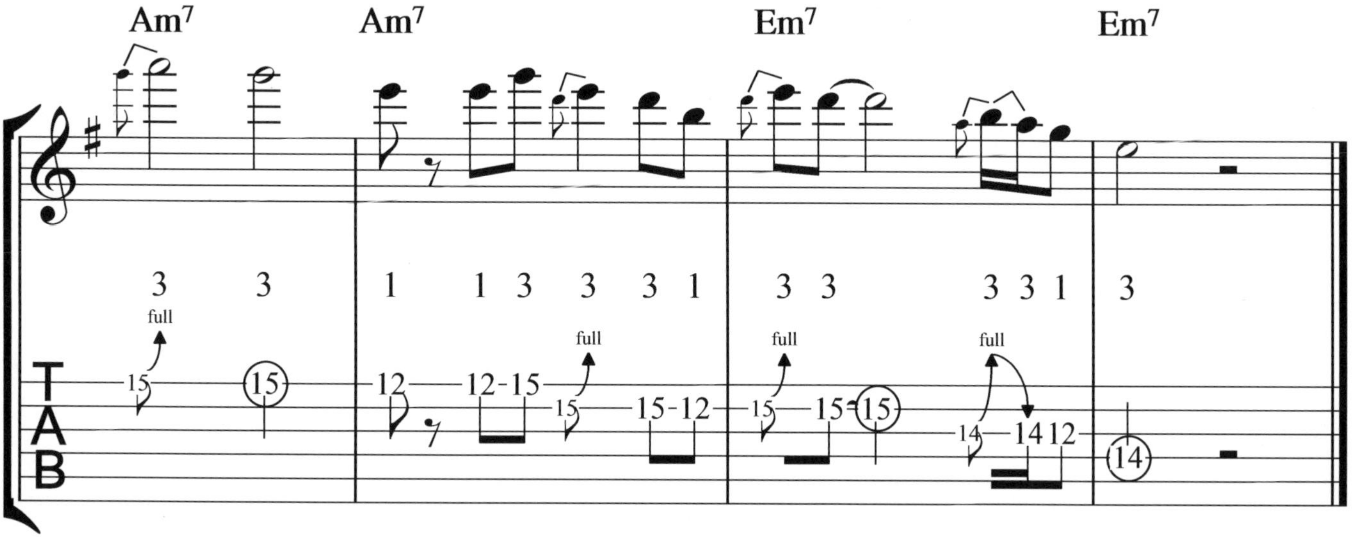

Jimi Hendrix Style Ballad Solo 2

Here's another 16 bars of the guitar solo inspired by Jimi Hendrix's slower ballad style songs. I'll provide detailed instruction on how to play each section of the solo with special emphasis on the more advanced techniques.

Phrase 1

Notice the whole step bend and release in the second bar. Listen to the Video for more information.

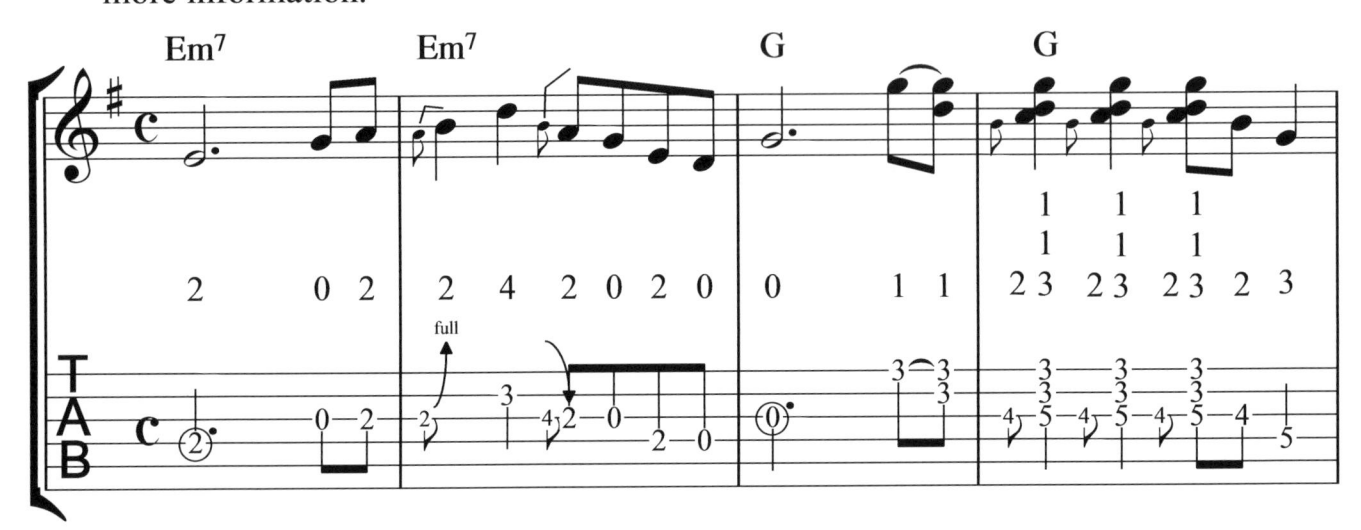

Demo

Each phrase will be played along with a backing track at the correct speed.

Trading Licks

Each lick will be traded back & forth. I'll play it first, then leave space for you to play it right after so you can compare your tone, timing, and articulation. Take your time and work on this section until you can play it perfectly all three times through.

Video & Audio Access

To Access Audio & Video for this course, go to this web address:
http://cvls.com/extras/jhs/

Phrase 2

Start on beat 2 of bar 1.

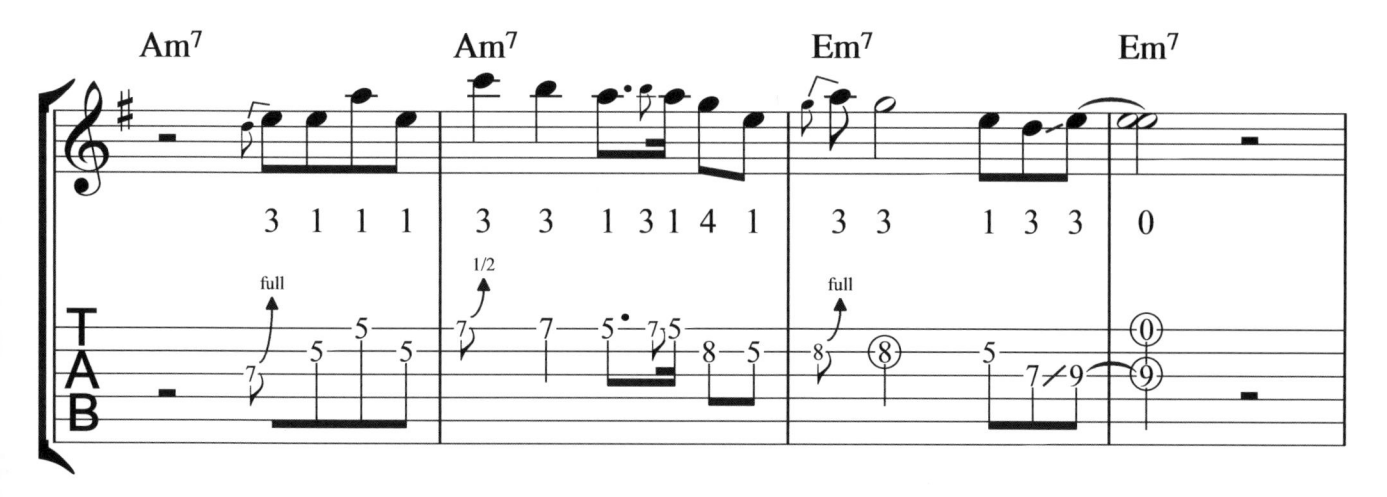

Phrase 3

This is similar to Phrase 2, but starting higher up the neck.

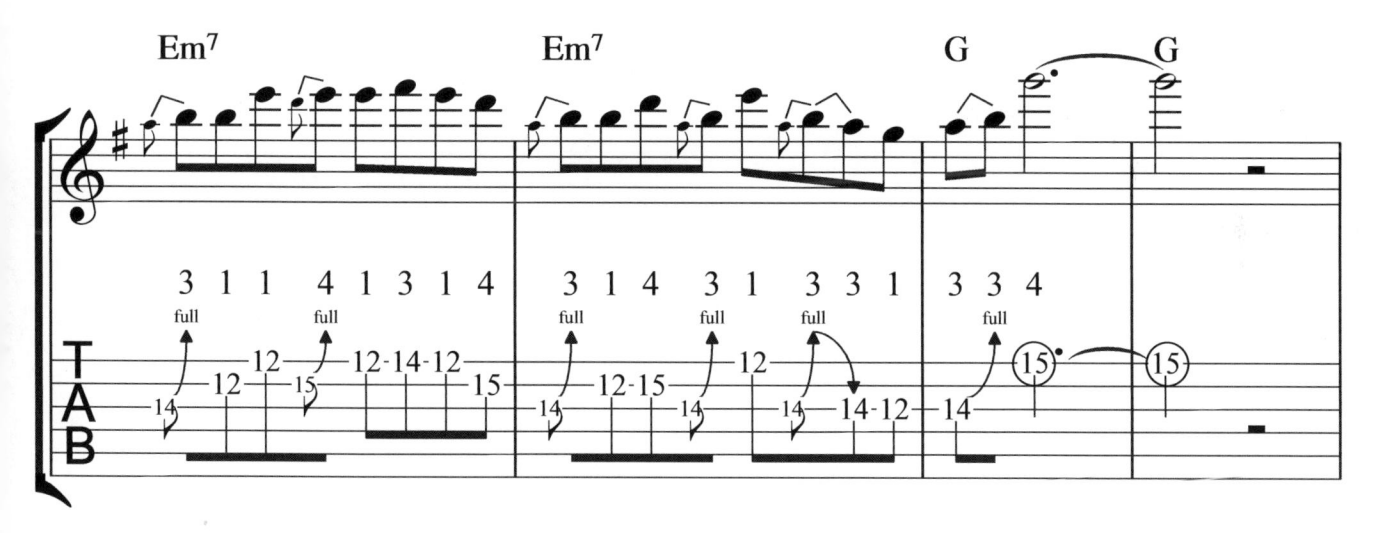

Phrase 4

This phrase uses compound bends and a series of triplets. Listen to the Video for more information.

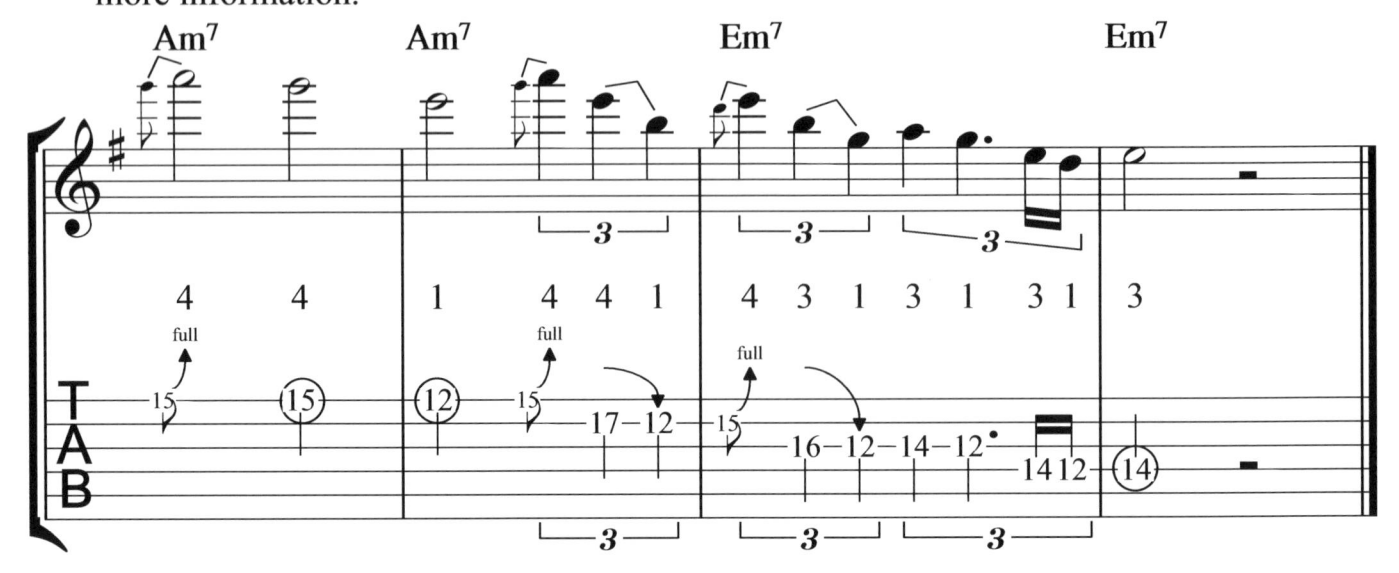

Playing With The Jam Track

Play the complete solo along with the jam track. You can access the file from the following web address:

http://cvls.com/extras/jhs/

Hendrix Style Ballad Solo 2

by Jody Worrel

Phrase 1

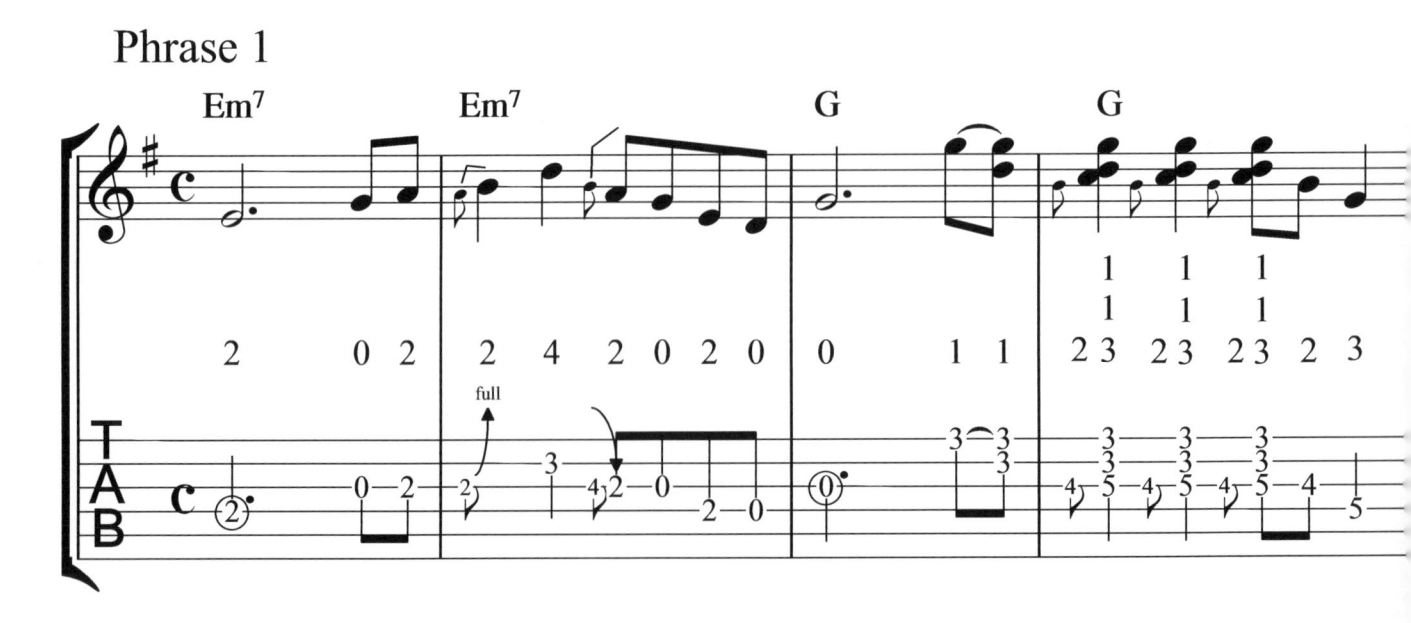

Phrase 2

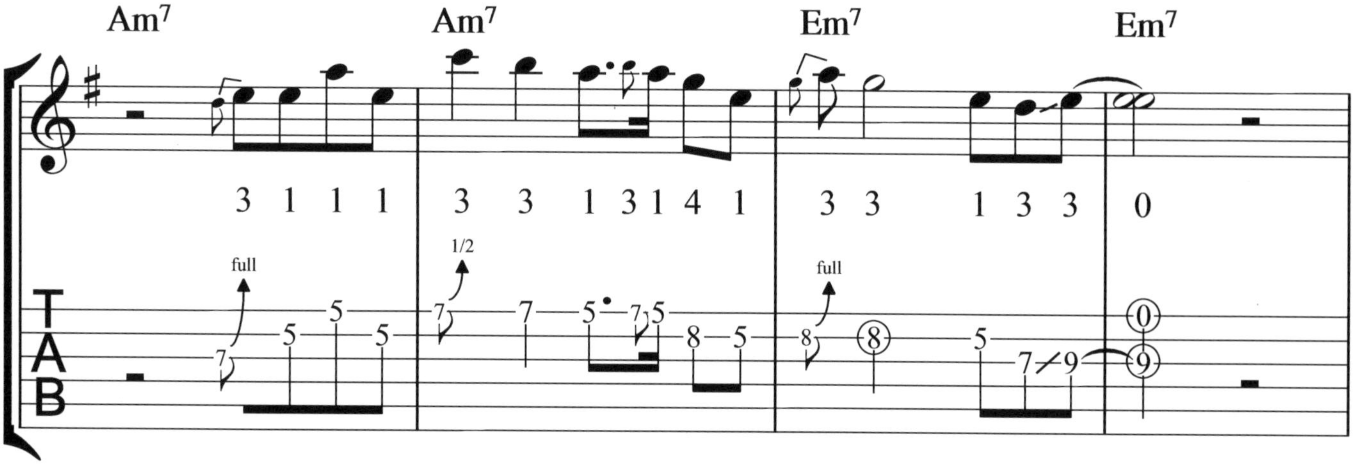

Phrase 3

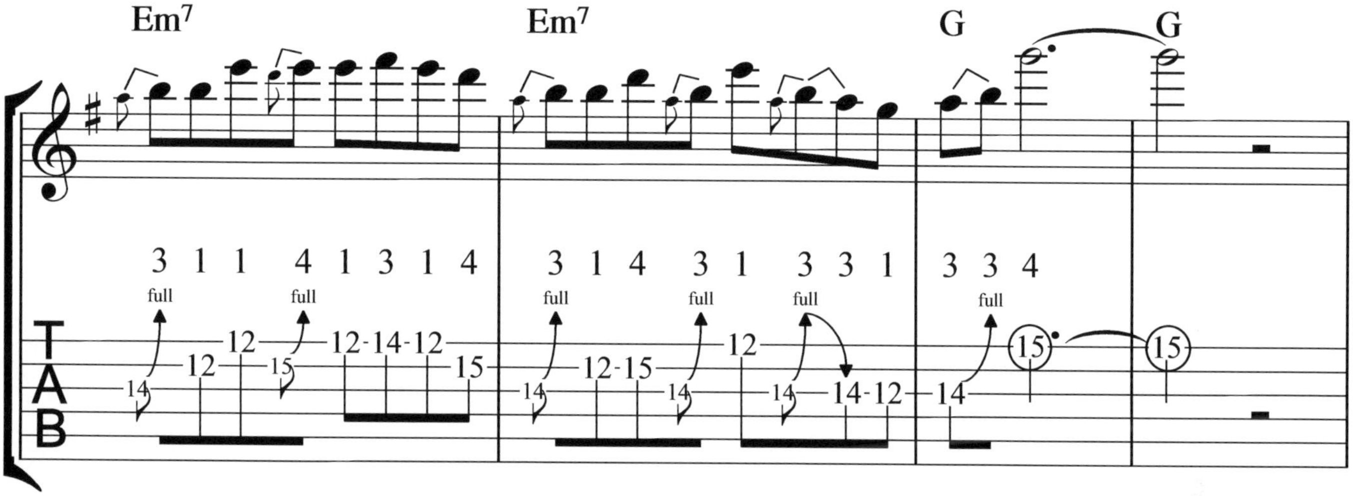

Phrase 4

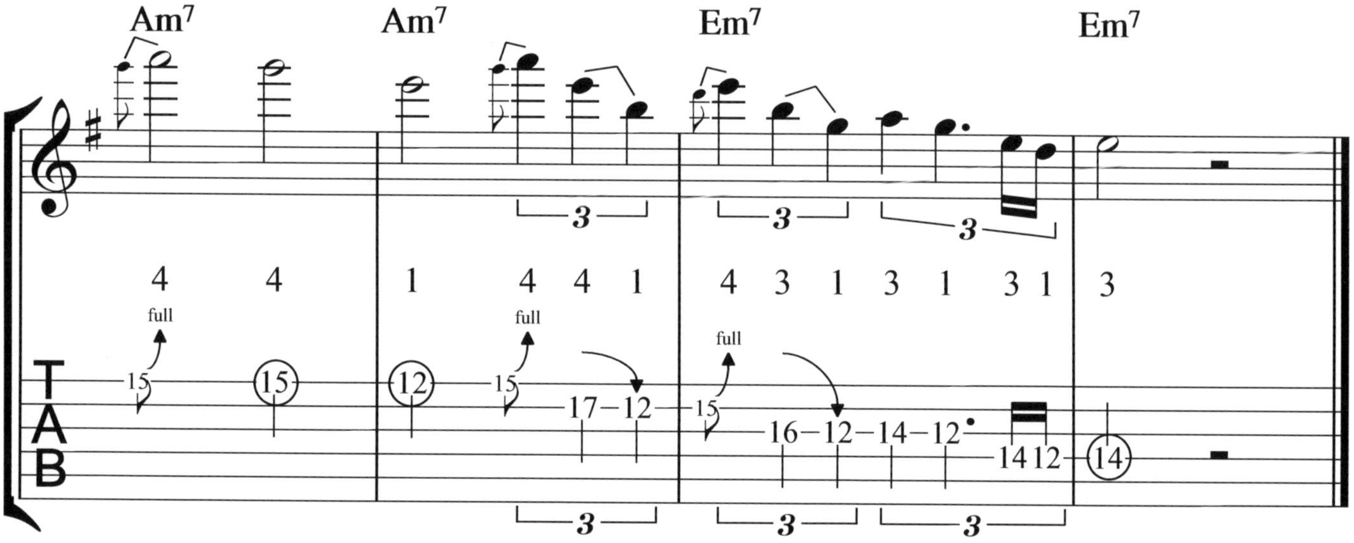

Jimi Hendrix Style Ballad Solo 3

This lesson covers 16 more bars of a solo in Jimi's soaring and dramatic style for ballads. Using note by note instruction, I will break down the solo into four smaller sections and explain how to play them in detail. You will get the opportunity to practice each section and the entire solo along with a rhythm track.

Phrase 1

Watch the Video for the prebend and bend and release in bar 3.

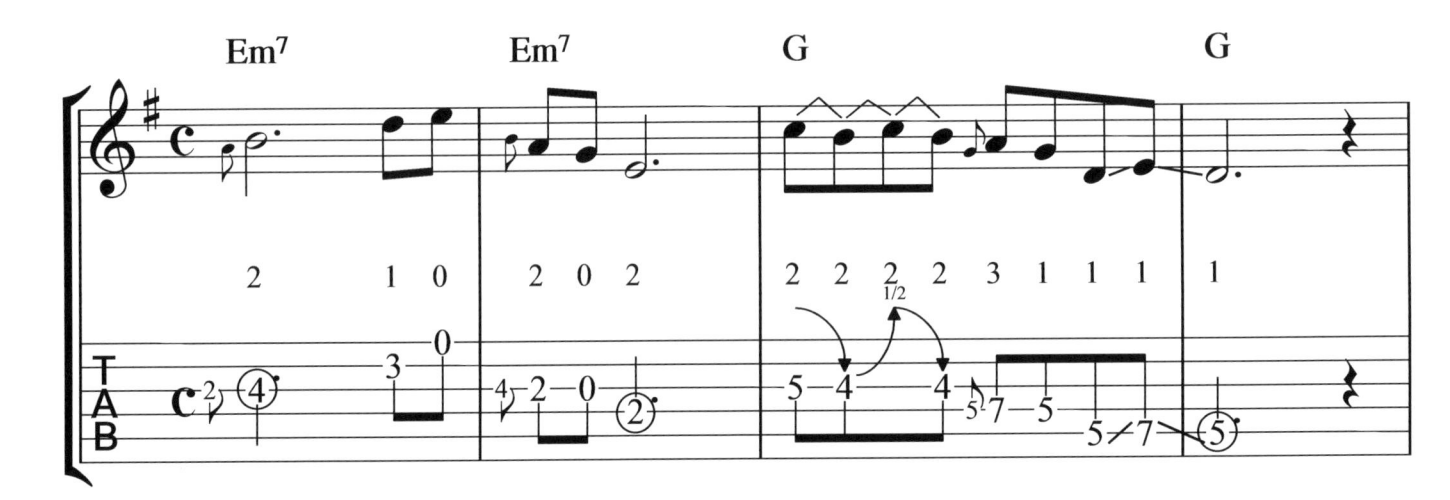

Demo

Each phrase will be played along with a backing track at the correct speed.

Trading Licks

Each lick will be traded back & forth. I'll play it first, then leave space for you to play it right after so you can compare your tone, timing, and articulation. Take your time and work on this section until you can play it perfectly all three times through.

Video & Audio Access

To Access Audio & Video for this course, go to this web address:
http://cvls.com/extras/jhs/

20

Phrase 2

Start with a big bend up to a C note.

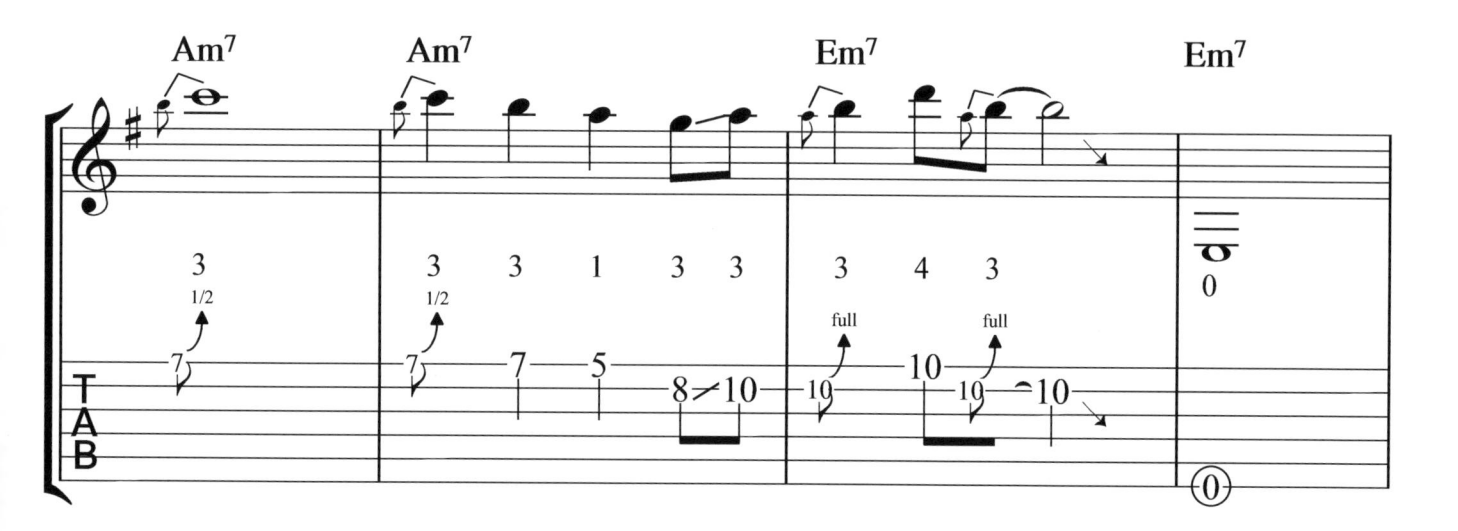

Phrase 3

This phrase uses pedal tones on the first string.

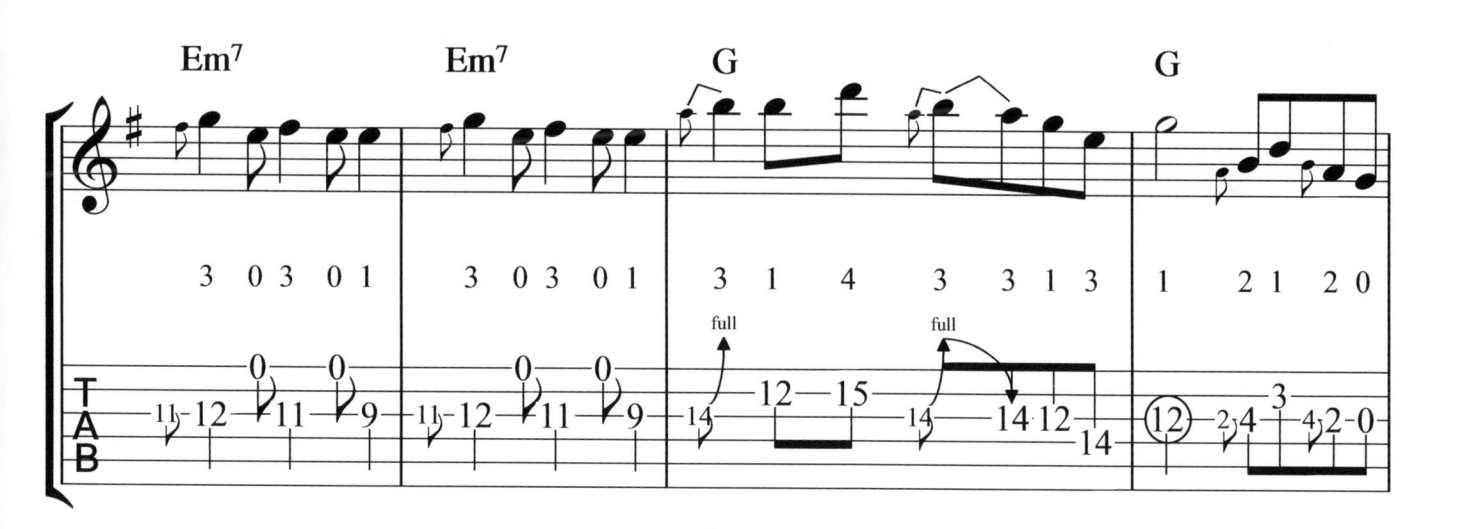

Phrase 4

This phrase starts with the last four eighth notes of Phrase 3.

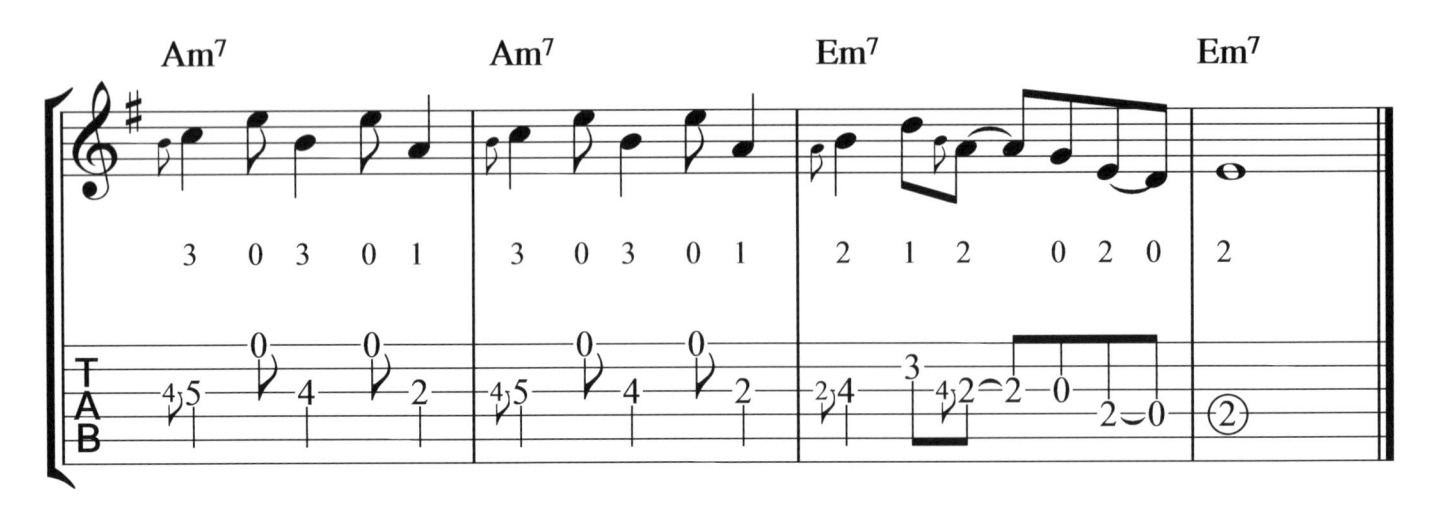

Playing With The Jam Track

Play the complete solo along with the jam track. You can access the file from the following web address:

http://cvls.com/extras/jhs/

Jimi Hendrix Style Ballad 3

By Jody Worrell

Phrase 1

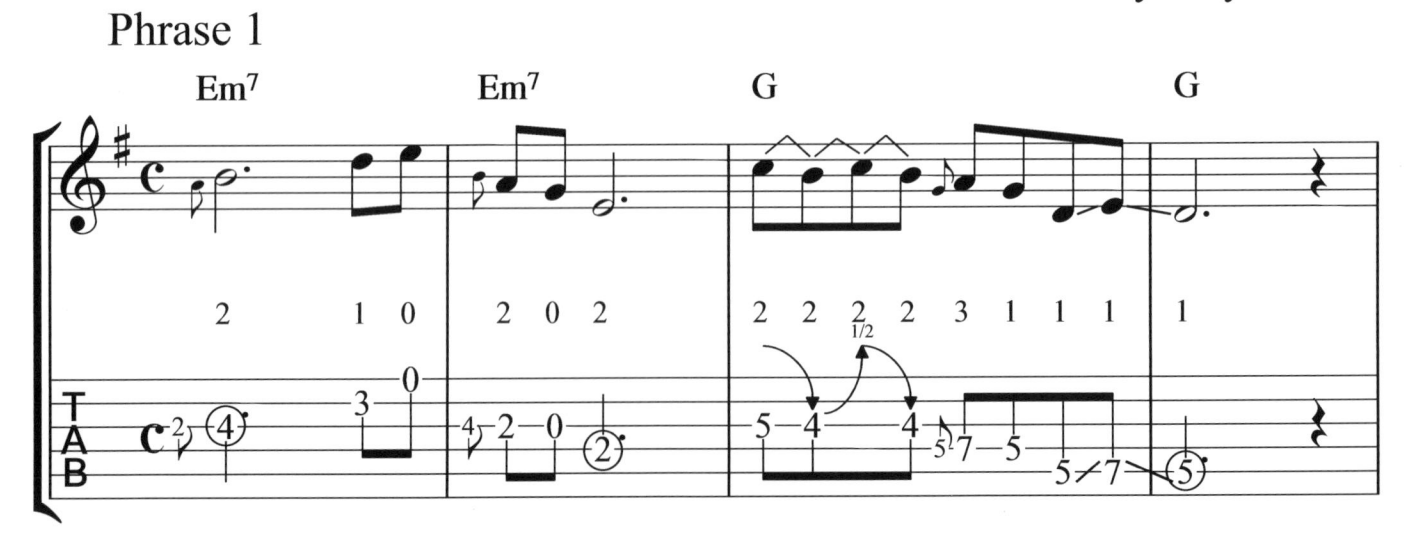

Phrase 2

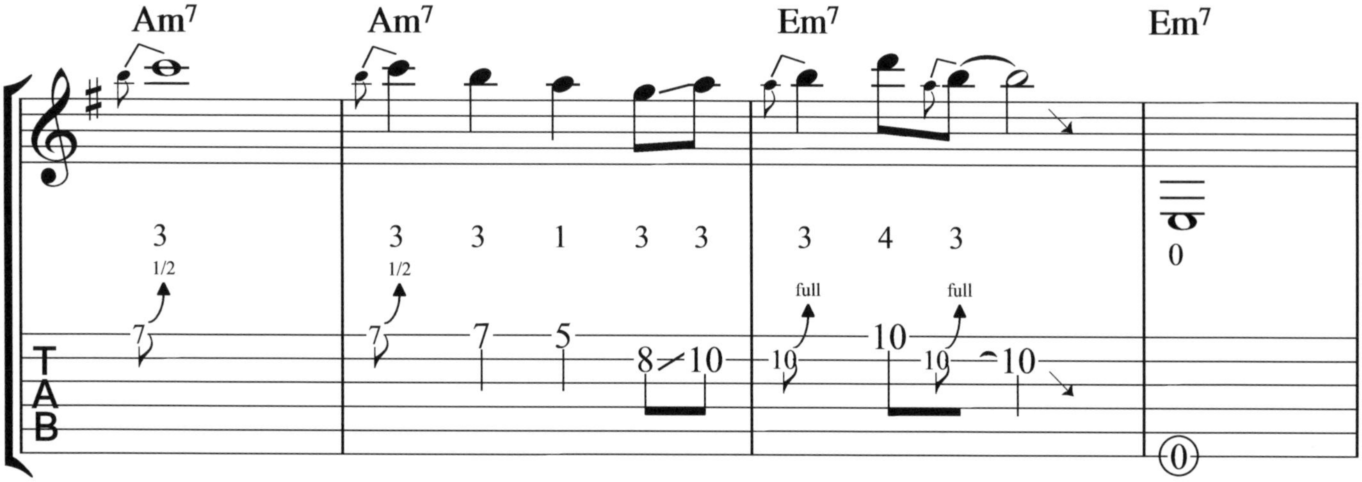

Phrase 3

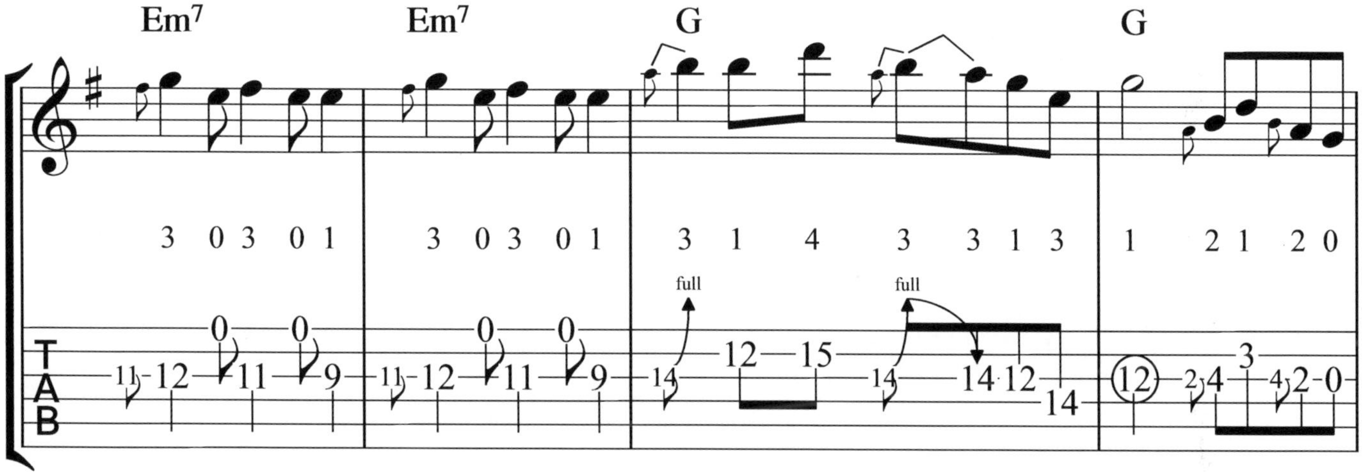

Phrase 4

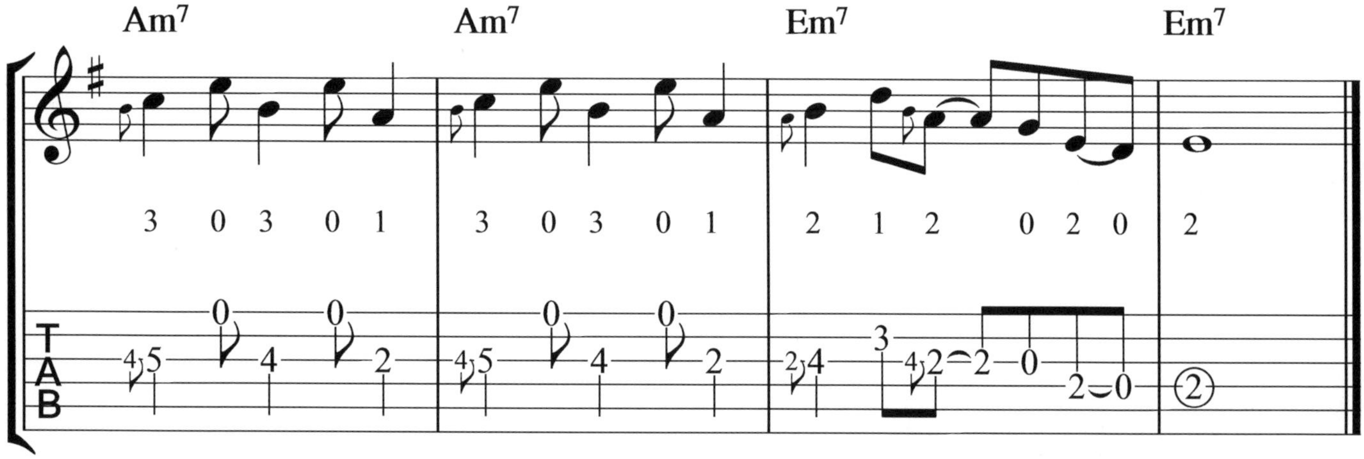

Jimi Hendrix Style Ballad 4

This will teach you a fourth solo in our lesson series that could be combined to play a 64 measure solo. I will guide you through the bends, vibrato, and other techniques that Jimi Hendrix used to create his legendary sound. I will break the solo down into four bar sections. You will learn how to play the solo note by note and get to practice with jam tracks that loop each section.

Phrase 1

This phrase starts out low on the 6 string.

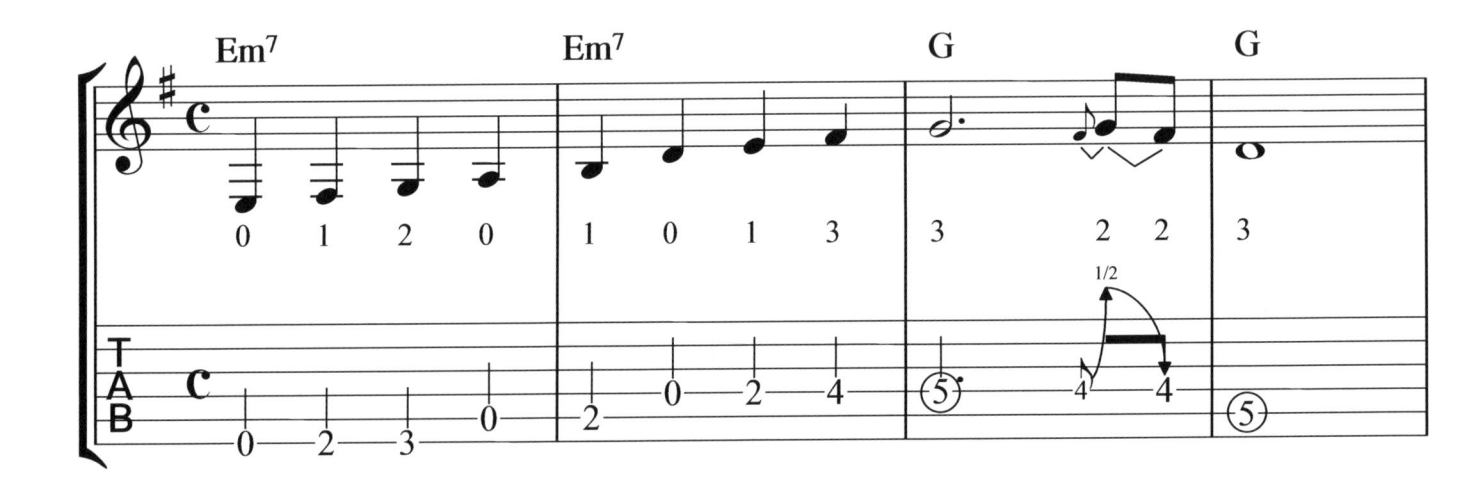

Demo

Each phrase will be played along with a backing track at the correct speed.

Trading Licks

Each lick will be traded back & forth. I'll play it first, then leave space for you to play it right after so you can compare your tone, timing, and articulation. Take your time and work on this section until you can play it perfectly all three times through.

Video & Audio Access

To Access Audio & Video for this course, go to this web address:
http://cvls.com/extras/jhs/

Phrase 2

Start with a half step bend for three beats (a dotted half note).

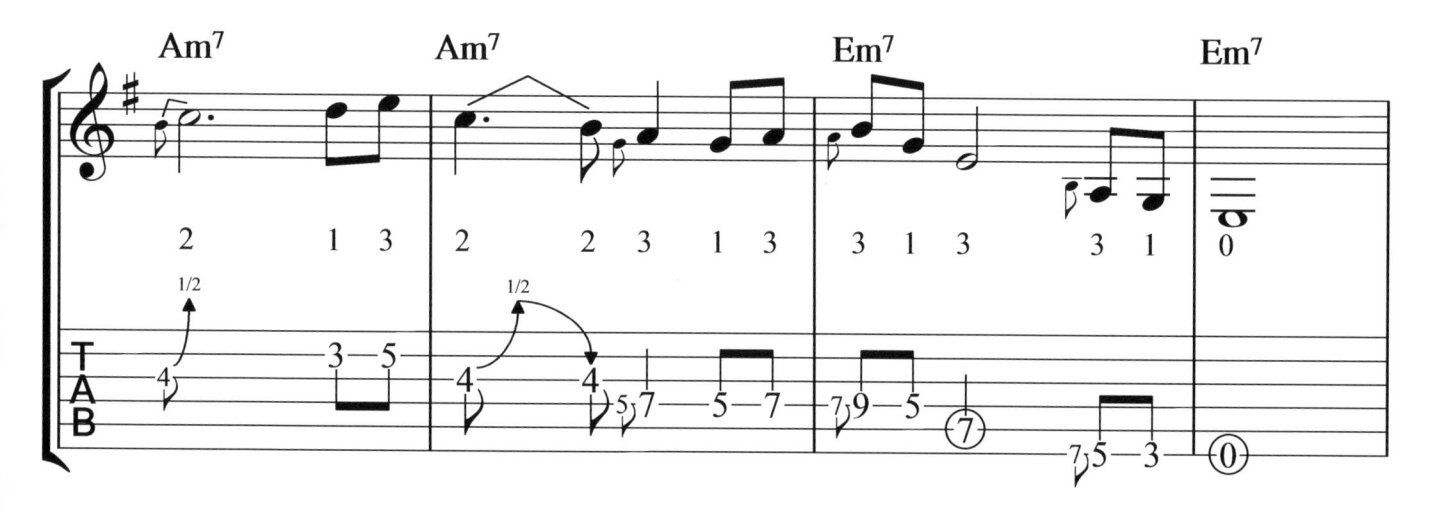

Phrase 3

Start at the 12th fret using the minor pentatonic with a familiar blues & rock lick.

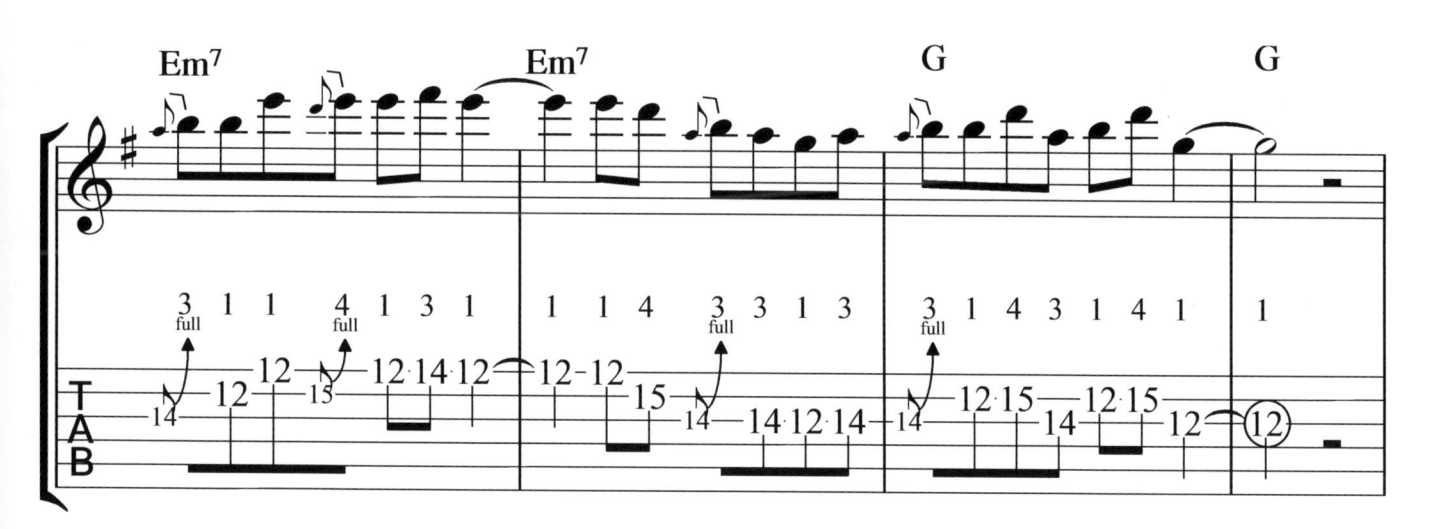

Phrase 4

Start with a majestic half step bend from the 12th to the 13th fret.

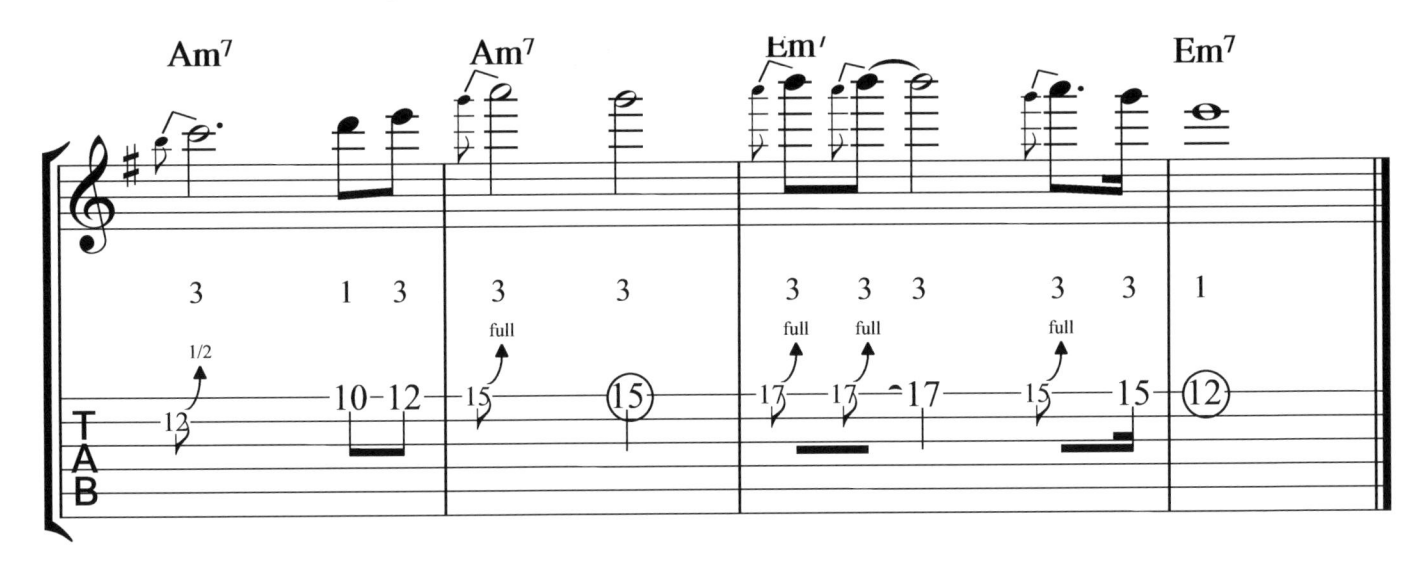

Playing With The Jam Track

Play the complete solo along with the jam track. You can access the file from the following web address:

http://cvls.com/extras/jhs/

Jimi Hendrix Style Ballad Solo 4

by Jody Worrell

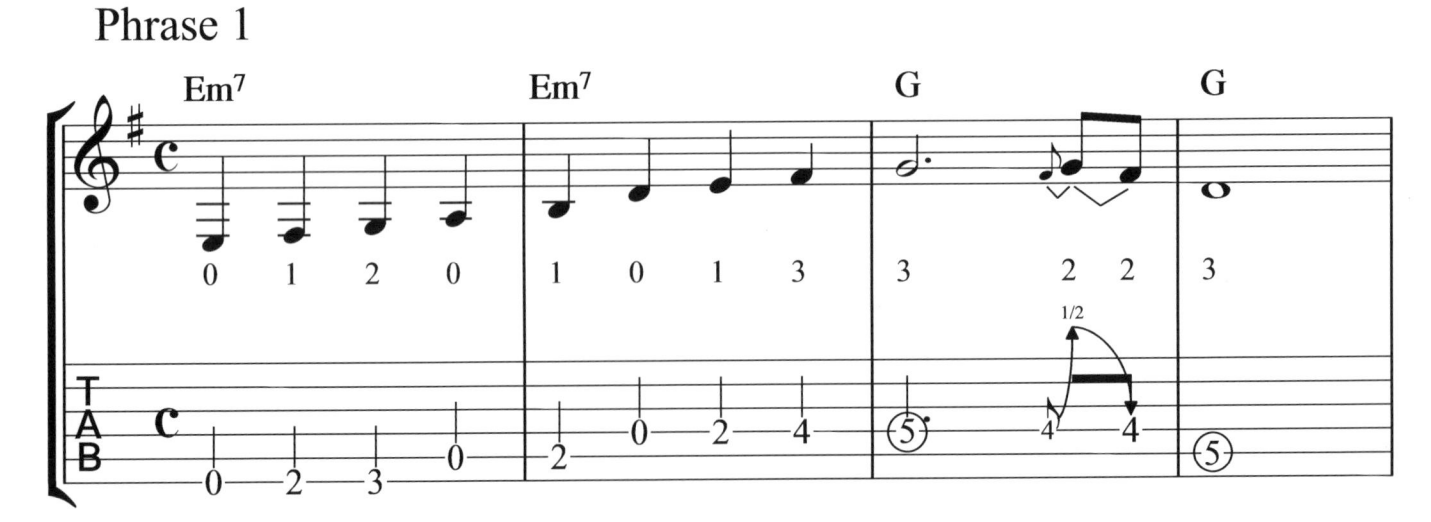

Phrase 1

Phrase 2

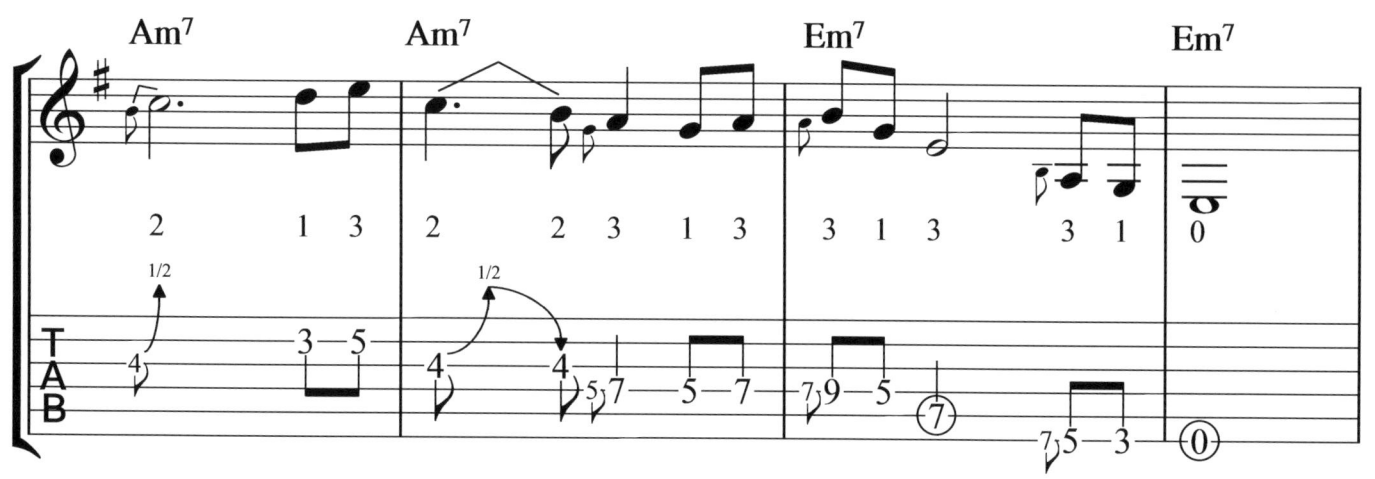

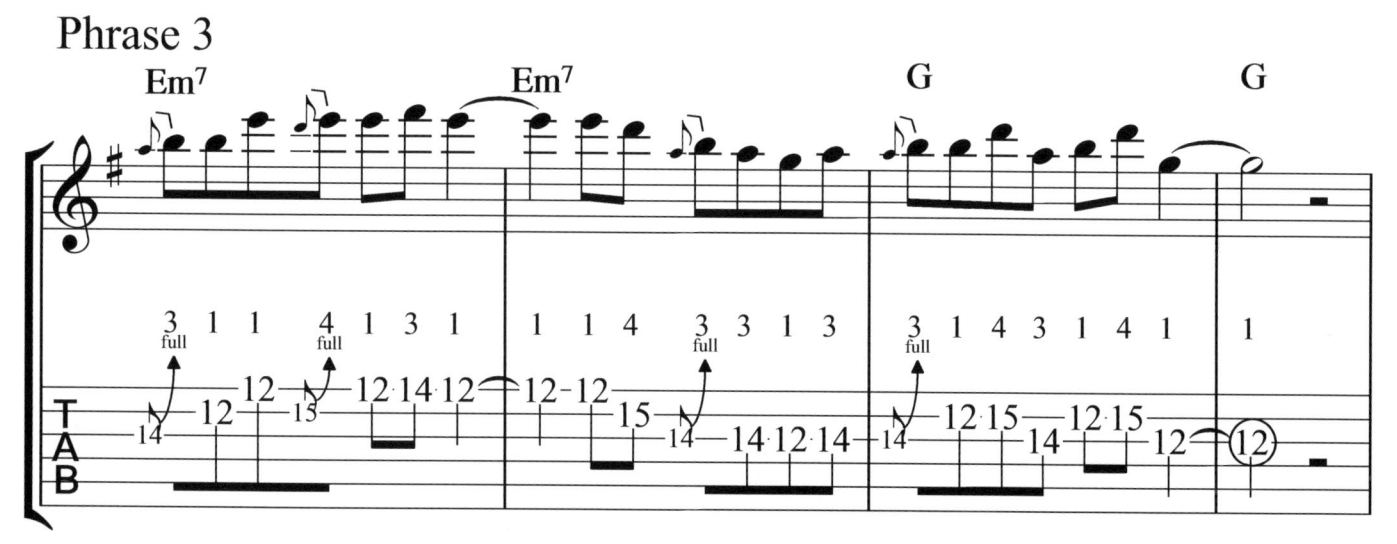

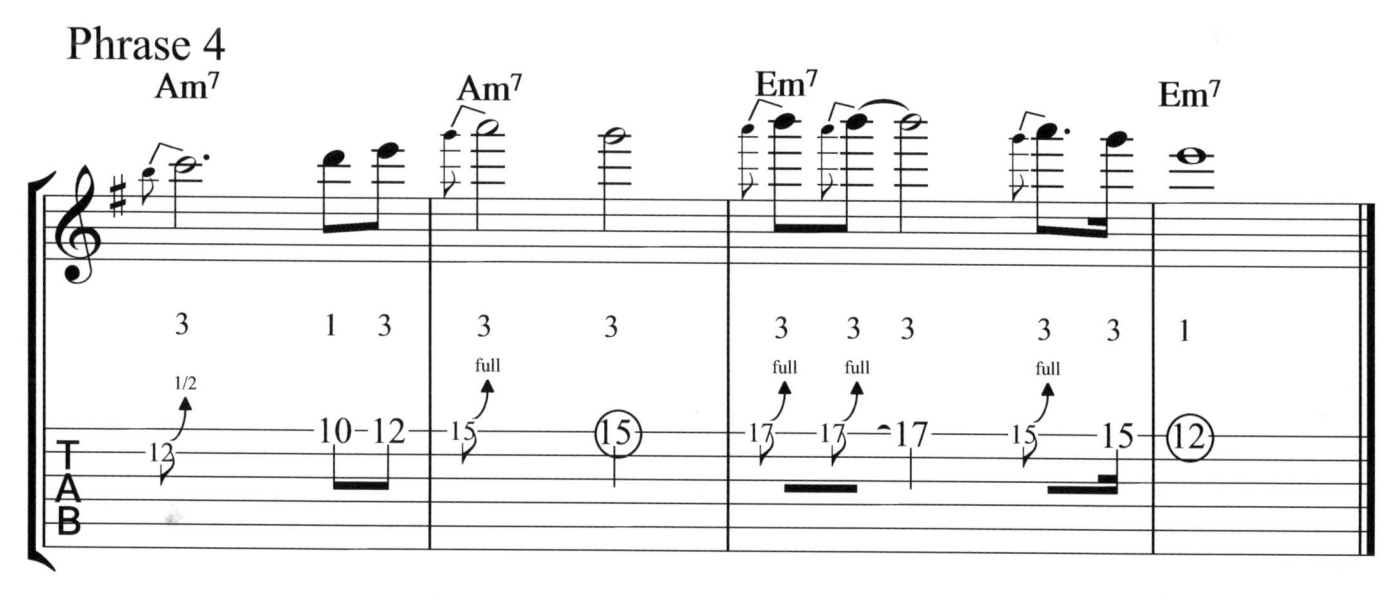

Phrase 3

Phrase 4

OTHER PRODUCTS IN THIS SERIES

The Stevie Ray Vaughan Style Guitar Book by Jody Worrell touches on the techniques and style that helped establish Stevie Ray Vaughan as a legitimate guitar hero. Jody will take you step by step through licks and solos teaching Stevie's approach to bends, slurs, hammer-ons, pull-offs, and note selection. After teaching you the lead parts, Jody will demonstrate them over a rhythm track. The included lessons are Stevie Ray Style Licks in A 1 & 2, Stevie Ray Swing Solos 1 & 2, and Stevie Ray Minor Solos 1 & 2. The package includes guitar tabs, 151 minutes of video instruction, and audio jam tracks.

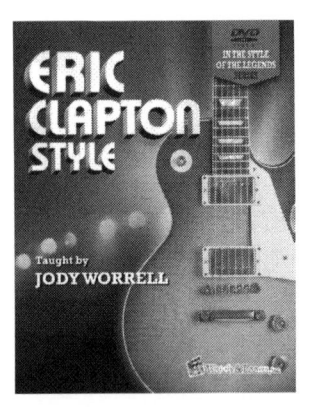

Eric Clapton Style Guitar Book with Video & Audio Access by Jody Worrell teaches the techniques and style that helped establish Eric Clapton as a legendary guitar hero. You will go step by step through the licks and solos learning Eric's approach to bends, slides, hammer-ons, pull-offs, and note selection. After learning the lead parts, they will be demonstrated over a full band rhythm track. Each lick or phrase will then be traded back and forth. Jody will play it first and leave room for you to play immediately after. This course includes online access to 2.5 hours of easy to use video instruction and audio jam tracks.

B.B. King Style Guitar Book by Jody Worrell teaches the techniques and style that helped establish B.B. King as a blues legend. You will learn the timing, note selection, bends, vibrato, and famous box position that all combine to create B.B.'s unique phrasing. After learning the lead parts, they will be demonstrated over a full band rhythm track. Each lick or phrase will then be traded back and forth. Jody will play it first and leave room for you to play immediately after. The package includes guitar tabs, over 3 hours of video instruction, and audio practice tracks for each lesson.

Pink Floyd Style Book by Jody Worrell teaches the techniques and style that helped establish David Gilmour as a rock legend. You will learn the timing, note selection, bends, and vibrato that all combine to create David's unique phrasing. After learning the lead parts, they will be demonstrated over a full band rhythm track. Each lick or phrase will then be traded back and forth. Jody will play it first and leave room for you to play immediately after. The package includes guitar tab, over 2.7 hours of video instruction, and audio practice tracks for each lesson.

Printed in Great Britain
by Amazon